Across *the* Kitchen Table

A Mother and Daughter
Turn Tragedy into Peace

CARLA SEAQUIST

SHE WRITES PRESS

Copyright © 2025 Carla Seaquist

All rights reserved. No part of this publication may be reproduced, distributed, or transmitted in any form or by any means, including photocopying, recording, digital scanning, or other electronic or mechanical methods, without the prior written permission of the publisher, except in the case of brief quotations embodied in critical reviews and certain other noncommercial uses permitted by copyright law. For permission requests, please address She Writes Press.

Published 2025

Printed in the United States of America

Print ISBN: 978-1-64742-730-6
E-ISBN: 978-1-64742-731-3
Library of Congress Control Number: 2024917234

For information, address:
She Writes Press
1569 Solano Ave #546
Berkeley, CA 94707

Interior design and typeset by Katherine Lloyd, The DESK

She Writes Press is a division of SparkPoint Studio, LLC.

Company and/or product names that are trade names, logos, trademarks, and/or registered trademarks of third parties are the property of their respective owners and are used in this book for purposes of identification and information only under the Fair Use Doctrine.

NO AI TRAINING: Without in any way limiting the author's [and publisher's] exclusive rights under copyright, any use of this publication to "train" generative artificial intelligence (AI) technologies to generate text is expressly prohibited. The author reserves all rights to license uses of this work for generative AI training and development of machine learning language models.

Names and identifying characteristics have been changed
to protect the privacy of certain individuals.

Across
the
Kitchen
Table

For my brothers,
J.C. ("J") and Ted

"The longer one hesitates outside the door,
the more estranged one becomes."

—*Franz Kafka*

"Life is easy to chronicle,
but bewildering to predict."

—*E. M. Forster*

Contents

Introduction

D ear Mom,
　Four or five years before you died—before advanced old age really did render everything "minus, minus, minus" for you—you asked me, in your typically point-blank way, "How will you write about me?"

With my typically vivid recall, I can replay our exchange.

It was a beautiful fall day, and knowing you loved the fall colors, I called you up and said, "Let's go for a drive."

In the hour it takes . . . I have to get used to this. With you gone, my verbs should now be past tense.

In the hour it took me to drive to you, you had prepared yourself to ask this question. I knew, because you were quiet when you got in the car and you weren't looking at the fall colors.

We drove west on the Old Pacific Highway, and at the bend in the road that skirts the tiny town of Adna, you asked me. I was not surprised; I had been waiting for it. Your question did two things. It acknowledged the struggle between us that had endured so many years—four-and-a-half decades—but it also nodded hopefully toward the important rehabilitative work we— you and I—had done in the dozen years since I had returned with Larry to your orbit. Even then I was starting to hear the "minus,

3

minus, minus" from you when I called every evening to ask how you were doing. I knew you were putting your affairs in order, and this affair—our struggle—was the biggest.

Early in our rehab, we were playing double solitaire, and I said to you, laughing, "You know, Mom, this mother-daughter thing between us is *the* main event."

Slapping down the winning card, you said, "You betcha."

So on our drive, you wanted to know my final verdict about you, about us.

"All good things, Mom," I said, my heart warming to you in a way I had not felt since I was a little girl enchanted with my beautiful mother who could do absolutely everything.

I realize now I could have said, "*Only* good things," and perhaps been even more reassuring to you.

But that moment felt like another one of our ultraviolet moments we'd achieved in those years of rehab, when, sifting the past, we came to a divisive memory. We'd step into the ultraviolet light together and only truth fell from our mouths, unedited. "All good things, Mom," I said, unedited, and I reached over and took your hand. With tears in my eyes, my heart bursting, and one hand off the steering wheel, I had to make an effort to mind the road while minding this culminating moment.

"Do you realize, Mom, how big a thing it is that we—you and I—have accomplished? Do you have any idea? It is enormous, it is profound. In the context of eternity—"

I felt you brace with your thought: *Carla is getting intellectual.*

"No, really, Mom, stay with me here. The ancient Greeks—all drama begins with the ancient Greeks—they wrote plays about families, *and they were all tragedies. Tragedies.* There was Electra who killed her mother Clytemnestra . . ."

You braced again. "She killed her mother? That was extreme, wasn't it?"

"Yes, it *was* extreme, but it shows how deep these conflicts in the family can go. The crazy-making, blinding, vengeful anger. And there's more. Electra killed her mother Clytemnestra *because* Clytemnestra had killed Electra's father Agamemnon *because* he'd sacrificed Electra's sister, Clytemnestra's daughter, Iphigenia. The whole *Oresteia* trilogy is about a family tearing itself apart, taking revenge on each other—not able to talk, not able even to see each other. But you and I, Mom: We forgave each other. We turned tragedy into peace. *This does not happen*—not in drama, not in history, not in life. But I was just *so* determined *this* mother and *this* daughter would *not* end in tragedy. Mom, I can't tell you how proud I am of us. Congratulations, Millie and Carla!"

For once, you didn't think your "artsy" daughter was overdoing it.

"Really now," you said. I saw you relax.

Never demonstrative, you purred, "Hmmm" as I recounted our various ultraviolet moments achieved in our rehab, announcing after each one, "Conflict resolved. Conflict resolved. Conflict resolved." By then we were at Rainbow State Park, farther down the road than planned. I turned off the road, into the park, and discovered a roadway leading to a new housing development. In your increasing isolation, you hadn't known it existed, and as you fixed your attention on the new dwellings, you returned to your true comfort zone—the pragmatic, the everyday. You couldn't stay in lyric mode for long.

But I can.

To prolong the moment a bit longer, I asked you for your verdict. "In all those years of struggle between us, when you thought I was opposing you just to be defiant, I really wanted harmony between us. You believe that now, don't you." I said it as a statement, not a question.

And you said, as a statement, "I believe you, Sissie."

Finally: anointment! When I got home that night, I said to

Larry, "It was *so* worth it moving back out here. Let me tell you the miracle that just happened."

It's been ten months now, Mom, since you left this earth. You often said, invoking the Lord, "He has written the hour of my death." It turned out to be January 22, 2018, a Monday, at 2:35 p.m.

It is fall now, a lovely time, like that day when we took our culminating drive. The tears have stopped, the analytic mind has returned, I am ready to tell our story.

Apart from my oceanic love for you—it would have been nice to feel this feeling for you earlier, but I will take it, even if late— there's an abundance of prompts to aid me in the telling. Your cremains are still in our kitchen, in a pretty ceramic urn in a shopping bag, cushioned by your favorite needlepoint pillows. We plan to inter you next year on your wedding anniversary, April 22, next to Dad. Until then, it's comforting to have you around. And your things—the good silverware and china, the antique tureens, and your jewelry—are on the island in our kitchen and in open boxes in the family room and garage. I thought I'd assimilate your "stuff" into the household as I wrote our story. For now, everywhere I look, I see a memory.

You came to see the usefulness of telling our story . . . not at first, because you thought such things were private, but ultimately.

As you said, while observing the increasingly unhappy state of the world and "all the clashing" in relationships portrayed on TV, in the movies, and in families we knew: "I think the world could use a story of conflict resolved."

I would only want to write about conflict *resolved*.

Long ago, Dad said to me, "You should write about Mom and you."

"Only if we get a happy ending," I said. Writing only about the hurt and hurt unresolved always struck me as a fraction of the story—only Part One and only the writer's hurt, nobody else's.

Introduction

Memoirs like *Mommie Dearest*, the screed by Joan Crawford's daughter, seemed exploitative and weaselly to me, not worth the big sales or notoriety.

On a higher plane but still a rant, there is Franz Kafka's *Letter to His Father*.

For a play I wrote about Kafka, I read everything he put to paper. In his *Letter* he ranted about his tyrannical father.

"From your armchair you rule the world." He complained about his father's incessant stories that "positively have worn grooves in my brain, such as, 'When I was only seven, I had to push a barrow from village to village.'" He was ever anxious about "this terrible trial that is pending between us." It was Kafka's tragedy that he could not cancel that trial, could not see his father as a boy pushing that barrow. It was only later, when his tuberculosis became terminal, that Kafka—too late—came to see his father as an "errant brother, scapegrace son." As a human being. You appreciated the part about "errant brother, scapegrace son."

So, Mom, I pledge, in this accounting, to portray your humanity in full, along with my own. I canceled our trial long ago. You often said to me, angrily and accusingly in our bad times, jokingly in our good times, but always (I will acknowledge) quite accurately, "You always have to have the last word, don't you?"

Yes, I do. I believe in the authority of my word, because it was so hard fought for in a moral and mortal battle with you, my mother and my moral arbiter. Our battle being moral, about right and wrong, I had to engage with all my conviction and powers, no matter my fears and anxiety. In a moral struggle lasting decades, one has time enough to rethink one's position, but I never found my position in the case of Carla v. Millie to be invalid.

Yes, I will have the last word with this memoir. But the glorious thing is, because we found each other again and because we settled all our arguments to our mutual and frankly surprised satisfaction, the last word here is not just mine. The last word here is ours . . . yours and mine, together.

As I sit down to write our joint memoir, I have so many feelings—gratitude, pride, relief—that our primal relationship between mother and daughter has been set aright.

That is not to say our relationship wasn't—isn't still—the most complicated relationship in my life, by many magnitudes of difficulty.

I can hear you say, "Same here!"

This is also to acknowledge our reconciliation was mostly at my lead, and to get there, I deployed every technique at my disposal—diplomacy, psychology, and humor—and dug deep into reserves of patience I did not know I had.

But, bless you, Mom, you stuck in there with me, all the way. In all, we had seventeen years of Renaissance together.

One last thing before we start. In the aftermath of your death, I heard from many friends who conveyed thoughtful condolences.

One wrote, "Your task now is to work through the ultimate separation."

And of course several wrote that, with both parents gone, I was an "orphan." All true, and yet having achieved, finally, a profound connection with you only in these last seventeen years—a connection I longed for during decades of alienation—I am still feeling it: the connection that you and I enabled by opening up the channel so long dammed between us.

Human beings want to talk to their beloveds in the beyond, notwithstanding the "ultimate separation." I rejoice that I can do that now. I can talk to you in my heart. Finally, because of our endeavors, the channel is open and the signal is clear.

Several months ago, when I could trust myself to read the many thank-you notes you sent us after yet another family get-together we organized, in one note you wrote how happy you were to tell your friends that, "Ever since Carla returned, our relationship has 'blossomed'" and how happy you were that, at long last, we could "express ourselves to each other." I ran downstairs to Larry, read those words to him, and bawled a happy bawl.

E. M. Forster said, "Only connect."

We finally did. That's all I ever really wanted . . . for us to connect, to communicate.

And what is a more personal means of communication than a letter, this one I am about to write?

Let's do this, Mom. I will continue speaking to you here in the way I did the last year-and-a-half of your life, in assisted-living facilities, when I would recap for you, rather like a documentarian, the highlights of your life, of our life together as a family. You liked that kind of "You Are There" storytelling. You would nod at a recollection and look at me and smile. Most gloriously, with my arm around you, you would lean into me, listening closely . . . the loveliest way possible for our particular story to end its earthly chapter.

Part One

The Early
Years

"In a nutshell"—one of your favorite phrases—our problem was this:

As a preteen, it became my sense of things that you treated Dad more and more harshly, for what reason, it wasn't clear. Thus, it was my responsibility, as the eldest child and a developing moral being, to step between you two, defend Dad against your harshness, and try to bring you two to make peace. It was the right thing to do morally, defending Dad against your bullying. But emotionally, it meant losing your trust—a terrible, terrible loss. (I feel nauseous now, recalling it.)

You began to look at me with suspicion, hurt, and even, it seemed, hate. Doing the right thing morally also meant losing the warm mother-love I had luxuriated and basked in as a bright and happy child. Suddenly you turned cold; suddenly I *was* an orphan, even though both my parents were alive.

In turn, you lost my warm daughter-love. I couldn't "love you up" anymore. I tried many times over the ensuing decades to rekindle our relationship and free us from our tragedy, which came to feel as grievous as any Greek tragedy of old. But you continually resisted.

"You always favored your father, never me" and "It's past, I said. Leave it!"

Our struggle began when I was in seventh grade, at age twelve, after early years that were near-idyllic. I say "near," because dark clouds had moved onto the scene when I was in second grade, when we moved from the countryside into town.

In those years out in the country, I was so enchanted by you, my beautiful mother. You were my sun, moon, and stars. A stay-at-home mom in today's parlance, you were not only there all the time, but you could do everything. You wrangled three small kids, all under the age of five, while Dad was establishing his medical practice.

You made all my clothes and yours, nothing store-bought, even turning Dad's old Army uniform into a playsuit for me. You even made our coats. There's a page in the photo album I assembled for you that displays your advanced handiwork on my behalf: two coats, my roller-skating outfit, and a beautiful party outfit that had a red-and-white striped underdress with an overdress of white organdy. I loved the dresses you made for my elementary-school years, with the pleating on the bodice and a Peter Pan collar.

You didn't stop there. You made the slipcovers for the sofa and curtains in all the rooms. And you clothed yourself so tastefully, you were the quintessence of "well-groomed." With your black hair and olive skin, you could wear any color . . . and did. If you slipped on your spectator pumps, you were one "snappy dresser." You aspired to "chic," which you pronounced "chick." Even (especially) during our years of alienation, I knew never to correct you about pronunciation. Your pride and your beauty were beyond critique.

Likewise, you made our meals from scratch . . . nothing packaged. You served from your own stores. You spent days in the summer heat canning peaches, pears, cherries, and apricots. You made blackberry, raspberry, and strawberry jams. You planted a vegetable garden with beans, peas, and tomatoes. You also planted a flower garden. I remember the poppies, the irises, the lilac bushes, and the "snappy-dragons."

You dedicated each day of the week to a specific task. Monday was for laundering clothes (and writing to your mother) and

Tuesday was for ironing. I can't remember the rest, but your week got filled.

After your mother died, you were "nagged" for years that on Mondays you had something else to do. "Oh yes. Write Mom."

You were a whirl of activity. *Mom, how did you do it all?* Last year, when you were in the assisted-living facility, after I related the above to the ladies at your dinner table, I turned to you afterward and asked quietly, "Was it too much work?"

You nodded. "Uh-huh."

Earlier during our rehab, you told me that in those first three years out in the country on the West Coast, you were "quite lonely," not only because in our part of Washington State there's the constant rain in the winter months, but also because you missed "your people," your family back in Ohio. But since you now had your own young family, you told me, "I put my head down and got busy." As a child, of course, I could not see the compensating going on, only the activity.

You also "got happy" by getting out and making friends. For a while, with no car, you were "stuck" and friendless. But soon enough we had two cars, both Studebakers—yours was navy blue, Dad's was light blue—and we went visiting.

My most vivid memory from those years: I am about four, not yet in school. We are in your car, I am seated in the middle, you are driving, and your new friend Peg Downey, wife of the manager of the J.C. Penney store in town, is in the passenger seat. It's a summer day, the windows are down, you are in a flowery dress, our hair is flying, and you are happy. You laugh, talk, and look over at Peg, all while working the gearshift *and* the foot pedals.

That's when the enchantment started. *Wow,* I thought, *my beautiful mother really can do everything.*

You made many friends. You had a real genius for friendship. The women you grew closest to were women like you, whose husbands fought in World War II and who were raising young children. These friendships were deep, both in the sense of deeply joyous and deeply serious. You became known for your vivacity.

I remember you cackling with your women friends in a wicked way that required me to be exiled.

"Carla Nan, this is not for you."

You and your friends could turn serious and talk about problems in the family, in the marriage, in life in general, and later, about widowhood. When a friend's husband left her for another woman, you spent a long afternoon in the kitchen, consoling her. You were the one sought out by others in trouble. You were admired for your level-headedness and good sense. However, you never shared what you talked about. You could keep a secret.

In the struggle to come between you and Dad, and you and me, you could not take our troubles to all your friends, since by then you were "leader of the pack." But I knew you consulted with a select few. They became your lifeline: Terry, Helen, and Marcie. And if you couldn't take it to your lifeline, you "took it to God," as you often said. You pondered things in your heart. As a precept to pass on to a child, taking responsibility for your own self, it was a good thing to see. But when, during the struggle with Dad, a call came in from one of your lifeline friends, the dichotomy between your warmth on the phone and your chilliness shown to us spoke volumes. It hurt volumes, too.

I remember when I was in high school, you received such a call. Dad shot me a hurt look, shrugged his shoulders, and looked away, his cheeks quivering. I thought he might cry. Now that I consider it, another reason I took up Dad's defense was because I knew he didn't have a lifeline of friends at his back nor a lifeline to God, like you did.

Out in the country, in those early years, I was such an ebullient child, so carefree. My God, Mom, I was a bouncy child. The home movies show me (and my ringlets) constantly in motion, like a piston, as I run in and out of the frame, jumping on my prone father's chest, then tearing off screaming with laughter. When you would lie down for a breather in the afternoons, I, not needing a breather myself, would bounce on your bed to get you back into the action.

I never took a nap. I was too excited learning about this thing called "life." You would put me down to sleep, but I used naptime to learn to braid my hair and tie my shoes and read my picture books, somehow expecting the stash of books under my blanket would escape your notice. In my exuberance, I also had a penchant for (I cringe to think of it) taking off my clothes and running around swinging my undies in the air. If I stripped in the front yard, a few honks of the horn from our farmer-neighbor driving past would alert you that your daughter was out making a public spectacle of herself . . . again.

You entered me in the Little Miss Chehalis contest of 1948, and I won. I was proud to be like my mother who'd been crowned Peony Queen of her high school. About that time, we modeled together in a mother-and-daughter fashion show.

I got even more excited about life when I learned to read in first grade. It felt like doors marked History, Literature, and Art swung open, beckoning me to walk through and learn. Naptime became totally impossible now. I began reading the magazines that came to the house—*Life, Time, Reader's Digest,* and *Ladies' Home Journal.* I even read the ones for Dad—*MD Magazine,* other medical journals, and from his wartime years, *American Legion.* I loved reading to my brothers, with J.C. next to me and Ted, an infant, sliding down my lap. I tried to stuff more knowledge into their heads because, as I saw from your active example, you needed to know things to acquit yourself in life.

In my exuberance, I loved to smooch my brothers and my father, running to greet him when he got home, and you, my beautiful, can-do-everything mother. Especially you. I could tell Dad was always a little surprised when I wrapped my arms around him. As you explained, he was an only child from an undemonstrative Finnish family, where displays of affection were not a usual thing. I made it usual, and from the family photos, you can tell he was happy.

My exuberance may have worn you out. As we discussed during our rehab, we both shared the same gene. When we got tired, we were useless. But my exuberance stemmed from this happy fact: I felt utterly safe and utterly secure. It wasn't just your serious demeanor that reassured me; it was the certain knowledge you, my mother, could handle anything that came our way. You were our Protector.

If we got sick, Mom the registered nurse cared for us. You often said the skills you called on most in motherhood were those you learned in nursing. One childhood disease of mine—I can't remember if it was measles, mumps, or chickenpox, but it was serious—you had to call another doctor. Dad was not available, which must have angered you, since he wasn't available for his own daughter. In my fever I recall you and Dr. Turner standing at the foot of my bed, speaking in low voices. You expertly followed doctor's orders and got me through. Given your expertise, it was a relief whenever you took a look at one of our playtime injuries and said, "Oh, it's nothing." We had to be very sick to pass your scrutiny and stay home from school.

In years to come, we all admired you when you nursed your father-in-law and your own mother through their final illnesses, and your own husband, Dad.

You also knew what to do in a crisis, like the earthquake of 1949. We were doing the breakfast dishes—you washed, I dried—when I noticed the cups in the cupboard suddenly swinging on their hooks.

"Mommy, look!"

J.C., climbing into his high chair, was thrown to the floor and started crying. You immediately grabbed both of us and ran out to the front yard, to safety.

Another time, you, me, and J.C. got caught in a snowstorm coming home from Portland. We were stopped at the bottom of a hill and could see, at the top, a truck hanging over the edge, having slid off the icy road. Later you said you felt the breath of your children on your neck.

"Are we going to make it, Mommy?"

We made it. We never saw you panic, cry out, or throw up your hands in helplessness. Never. You could cope. Always.

But my favorite image of you as My Protector, safeguarding me against the elements, emerged early. You enjoyed repeating it to me throughout my life, not just in those early years. When I was six months old, around the time World War II was ending, Dad was still stationed with the Army in Texas. You were living in a garage apartment when the landlady, a Mrs. Goodwin, banged on the door. You didn't like Mrs. Goodwin because you thought she took advantage of the desperate demand for housing and gouged you for rent (in the retelling you never forgot this detail). Banging on our door, she cried, "Quick, bring the baby, a tornado is coming!"

You grabbed me and ran along with her, taking cover in a ditch adjacent to a field. As the winds bore down on us, you covered me with your body. As you told it, I didn't like it "one little bit." I screamed and screamed. But the point is: My Protector protected me. It was the image I returned to incessantly, the image I missed most, when, during our later struggle, My Protector became My Opponent.

Where did your supreme competence and courage, your pride and self-reliance come from? You always pointed, proudly, to having survived the Great Depression while living on a farm in a small Welsh community called Venedocia in Ohio. Mingled with that pride was profound fear, which you did not disavow.

You spoke often of how, twice, the banker holding the loan on your father's farm came by to announce, "Well, John, I may have to foreclose on ya."

You were "terrified," you said, the only time I ever remember you admitting to terror. You described clinging to your father's pants leg and asking him afterward, using the expression you'd heard your parents use during those anxious times, "Are we going to be put out on the road?"

To save the farm and his family, Grandpa sold a prize pig. But you also could see fear made your father "a little crazy in the head." You did not scorn him for that. You said, "I could see how fear eats into you."

But for yourself, I'd say you determined, out of existential pride, to always "hold it together."

Consequently, from that harrowing experience, you absorbed deep into your bones the understanding that you, Mildred, were responsible for taking care of yourself.

As I said in my eulogy to you, "In many ways, the Great Depression never left Mom."

You were the ultimate self-reliant woman. You looked to yourself for a helping hand. You hated asking for help. I can't really remember when you did, except in the last year-and-a-half of your life.

You had a genius for economizing. You never threw food away, you saved every penny, you used towels until they shredded.

"Use it up, make it do, wear it out."

To save money, you cut our hair and, amazingly, your own.

To take care of yourself, you knew you needed a profession. With an endowment from your father of just $300, which was all he could scrape together in those tough times, you worked your way through nursing school. You became close with your fellow nurses Lois, Libby, and Helen and kept in contact with them all your life. You expressed pride in the quality of your nursing. Doctors wanted you to attend them in surgery.

You said, "I was a good nurse."

Around this time, shortly before the war, you met Dad in Cincinnati, where he was a medical intern and you were doing special nurses' training in tuberculosis. You met on a blind double date. It became family lore what your first impressions of each other were: Dad was "pleasantly surprised" that "the more beautiful gal" was meant for him, while you thought Dad was "sincere," not like the "hoity-toity" doctors you worked with. Romance blossomed.

When Pearl Harbor hit, Dad's first reaction was, "Well, I know where I'm going."

He was soon drafted by the Army and ultimately rose to become a captain in the Medical Corps. He left for Fort Ord, California, while you returned to your home area in northwest Ohio and were appointed the head of a small hospital—the appointment you noted with pride the rest of your life. Dad wrote you often, imploring you to join him in California. Finally you did, and you were married in 1942. You explained the reason you looked sad in your wedding photo with Dad was because your parents could not join you on that important day, which was conducted before a justice of the peace.

While Dad was overseas and would participate in the landing on Kiska in the Aleutian Islands, you worked, wanting to contribute to the war effort. Learning you could make more money as a driver "sitting on my fanny" than nursing, you chauffeured generals and drove a truck delivering equipment. You even delivered ammunition. You often cited a Captain Wright who trained you to back up your truck and stop on a dime. You always spoke of the war as a time when "we all pulled together," a high point from which the country has since fallen away.

While Dad was overseas, you journeyed by train to Aberdeen, Washington, to meet Dad's parents, arriving "filthy" from the long, hot trip. You often told the story of how Dad's mother was sick with worry about her only child sent off to war. She was a pacifist. She'd had a brother killed in war back in the old country and subsequently not only hated all war but uniforms of any kind (thus her son did not become a Boy Scout). It pleased you that you were able to calm her, by saying over and over, "Someone will survive this war and it might as well be your son." You were always glad you made that trip, because Grandma died not long after.

I came along December 1944 and J.C. in June 1946. As a new family, we moved to Washington State, where Dad had grown up and where his father, now widowed, still lived and worked as a longshoreman. That was the first "bone of contention" between you two. You felt you were "dragged" from your home in Ohio and "plopped" in alien territory. But, again, you got happy and adapted. You got busy and made yourself into the beautiful, do-everything mother I looked up to.

In the play *Mnemonic*, about memory and how it works, which I saw about twenty years ago, the narrator came onstage to begin the performance. Addressing the audience directly, he asked us to participate in a thought experiment. Roughly, it went as follows. My apologies to its creator, Simon McBurney, for the undoubted mix-up of my own memory.

> "Close your eyes," he said, "and visualize what you did today before you came to the theater. Easy to do, right?" (Strong affirmative from the audience.) "Next, visualize what you did earlier this week in chronological order, if you please. A bit harder, isn't it?" (The audience goes, "Hmmm.")

"Now, visualize what you did a month ago today. Where were you, what were you doing? Harder and harder, isn't it?" (Laughter ripples.) "Reaching back even further, visualize where you were five years ago." (The laughter grows louder.) "Ten years ago? Twenty years ago?" (Guffaws by now.) "Now, visualize yourself as a child, four or five years old. It is sunset. You are in a field with your parents. You hold their hands, Mother on one side, Father on the other." (The audience grows quiet and now purrs.) "Easy to do, right?"

Right. Easy to do. No doubt some in that audience, me included, had difficult relationships with their parents, with one or the other or both, but the sound coming from us, me included, was a general purr. It was acknowledgment of the foundational nature of the parent-child relationship. In that moment, whisked back to when I was four or five, I was again the happy, carefree, and secure child, holding the hand of my father, whom I'd later describe as resembling Jimmy Stewart, and my mother, whom I'd later describe as resembling Queen Elizabeth.

Enhancing that image, there actually was a field behind our house, where I loved to frolic. It was in that field I intuited the necessity of fences. In first grade, I'd somehow learned the word "aggrandize," which meant, as I inhaled it, to increase your stuff compared to the other guy. It came to me, in that field, that fences are needed to keep the other guy from aggrandizing himself at your expense.

Behind that field was an orchard of apple trees . . . yellow Golden Delicious. The neighbor lady, whom we called Grandma Elldee, said I could take home any apples that had fallen to the ground. It was there, in that orchard, our family made apple cider. You cranked the press while J.C. and I "helped" and you ladled cider into our mouths, the juice dribbling down our chins, the whole scene filmed by Dad.

Memory and how it works.

Of course, in the theater that night there was the inevitable one-two punch. Sorrow washed over me as I thought of that little girl holding her beloved parents' hands, and the storm coming at her and her parents in the not-so-distant future. Another wave washed over me as I thought of that cider-making. It was the last truly happy time for our family. It helped that the home movie Dad took of our family's last happy time together was cast in the amber glow of late afternoon.

Memory and metaphor.

Yet, I started to wonder. Given the power—the bone truth—of that foundational image of the little girl and her parents, evoked by theater, could we ever possibly recover the foundational connection in our current life? It existed once. Could it be rebuilt, breathed into existence again? Because it reflected exactly that little girl's state in those early years . . . happy and carefree and secure. All qualities soon to be lost.

Our move into town was necessitated by the arrival of Ted, the baby. Our house in the country was teeny. J.C. and I slept in one bedroom, and Ted was in a bassinet with you and Dad. We needed more room. You and Dad found a house in town, across from the elementary school, where you settled and lived for the next seventy years. Through the years there, you loved the sound of hundreds of children at play on the school's playground. The sound of the laughter and screaming "buoyed" you up. You made me promise, a number of times, that you would die in that house in your own bed.

It did not work out that way, Mom, and I am sorry.

You loved your new house, with the basement and attic having so much storage. You never changed the house's original yellow exterior color. Dad, with his fast-growing practice, spent his few free evenings paneling the attic and the basement and put in flooring and lighting. Again, you made all the curtains, even the heavier ones in the living room, organdy sheers everywhere else. I was your "help" in choosing the wallpaper, paint, rugs, and carpeting. The kitchen was L-shaped, forcing us to eat in a cramped nook, so you designed, expertly, an enlarged kitchen, squared out. At the built-in desk, armed with a phone, you organized dinner parties, our birthday parties, in short, you organized our lives. You called the kitchen "Grand Central."

Chehalis was the perfect hometown in the 1950s and '60s. It was small enough—never more than 5,000 population—that while you couldn't personally know everybody, you knew of them, of their family, their neighborhood, and their history. In this setting, people stood out as individuals and archetypes of the human parade, like the characters in Thornton Wilder's play *Our Town,* a play I love. Our little town, midway between Seattle and Portland, had the amenities of the city—good schools, good public library, movie theater, our own "Messiah" concert at Christmas—all without the posh attitude. If you gave yourself airs in Chehalis, you were hooted back to your regular self. The place was real. (Chehalis was hurt with the Walmart invasion in the 1980s, but it has fought back with typical "Bearcat spirit.")

You certainly never gave yourself airs, and as a doctor's wife, you might have. I especially admired you for that. You were not snooty; you were real. You made friends with "regular people," as you called them, as well as members of the Ladies' Auxiliary of the county medical association. As with any human settlement, there's a sociology of rank and status, but you crossed the lines every day and were widely admired for it. Our town's status line ran between the "hill people" and us down in the flatland—"Lower Slobbovia," as you called it. You didn't hesitate to pledge allegiance to the latter. Maybe that's why you never left the house without your hat and gloves. Pride. You and Dad always patronized local businesses (especially in the downturn), unlike the wives of other professional men in town, who'd "run up" to Seattle or "run down" to Portland for another acquisition in home furnishings.

A note about these women. A later generation would disdain the "ladies who lunch," who didn't work outside the home, but I remember these women who came to your lunches or played in your two bridge clubs as fascinating. These were the wives of bankers, lawyers, dentists, insurance brokers, lumber middlemen, car dealers, and other doctor's wives, many of whom lived up on "the hill," but some who lived in the new subdivisions. They arrived in hats and gloves, suits, fur stoles (Dad soon got you one of those), and heels, trailing White Shoulders perfume. I hung around these gatherings, taking in the talk about their children, their husband's work, and their charities. It was among these women I first saw wit displayed with a light remark or a story charmingly told, and I saw the pleasure it gave. The wits usually had "some college," as you explained later. You never indicated any inferiority to these women, with your nurse's training. Still, I wondered how much you enjoyed these gatherings, because after the last lady left, you'd invariably say, "Well, that's done."

Before they arrived, you sweated the details. I helped by coloring place cards and decorations. Once, trying to hurry me along, you grabbed a crayon and began coloring, but I objected. "No, Mommy, you have to stay *inside* the lines." Perfectionist vs. pragmatist.

Over time, I have become more pragmatic like you.

With your social ease, you soon became a pillar of the community, one of its engines. You organized blood drives. I remember you donning your old nurse's outfit, complete with cap and cape (all of which now hang in my closet, next to Dad's old Army uniform). You organized the Girl Scout cookie drive for years, starting even before you enlarged the kitchen. To get from garage to kitchen, we had to squeeze through a canyon of cartons. When you saw me sighing with envy about J.C.'s Little League experience, you organized a girls' softball league with four teams and ran it for several years; you were scorekeeper. You took up golf and won several club tournaments (and you had critical things to say about the women who spent too much time at the clubhouse, in post-game drinking and gossiping, when they should have been home with their children).

Of course you attended all our school activities—assemblies, plays, and sports events.

I remember a school assembly when I was in the fourth grade. All four grades sang in unison, "Roll On, Columbia, Roll On." What a "big sound" we made, you said; you were proud your daughter was featured playing the triangle. You made it your business to know our teachers. You always signed off on our report cards with a personal note. You attended parents' nights and PTA meetings, often alone because Dad was out making house calls.

As far as school went, you had no problem with me. The excitement I had about reading I had about school. I scarfed up the assigned reading, always did the extra credit reading, and wandered into related reading. I worked my way through the set of World Book Encyclopedias that you and Dad bought. My teachers would find essay contests for me to enter and advanced spelling books for me to consume. I was so loaded down, I tended to start researching and writing my term papers late, but I always aced them.

During my stellar high school career, you crowed once to Dad how my achievement was your doing. But Dad, in about the only time I can remember him contradicting you, said, "No, there's something about Carla Nan that drives her in her studies."

I didn't like it when you called me from my studies to set the table or help with the housework. Give me homework, not housework! It was the life of the mind that thrilled me. I know that hurt you.

Apart from school, I had other enthusiasms. In elementary school I went through the usual activities for the young, postwar bourgeoisie-like lessons in ballet, tap dance, baton twirling, and roller skating. In third grade, after I spent the summer on your parents' farm, I came home wildly enthusiastic about the piano, after watching my twin cousins playing duets and pointedly not telling me where Middle C was, the key literally to the kingdom. I ran back to Grandma's.

"Grandma, Grandma, where's this Middle C?"

Grandma urged you to get me a piano, because with her help I'd already taught myself to read music. You countered that Carla Nan had a lot of enthusiasms that she didn't stick with, but Grandma prevailed. You found me a used spinet piano, which, thank you, became my emotional lifeline during the tensions to come between you and Dad.

Several years later, when I was making real music, beyond exercises, Grandma and I were at a piano concert. I started crying in the second movement of Beethoven's "Waldstein Sonata," my first experience of the ineffable.

"Oh Grandma," I said, "it's *so* beautiful." Grandma, who would normally shush any "blubbing," let me cry.

After I ran through my first piano teacher in Chehalis, you found one in Seattle who agreed to come down one day a week, if you could find six or seven other pupils to make it worth his time. (You did.) You attended all my recitals and drove me to Seattle for my adjudications before a judge, bucking me up beforehand.

You knew the "iffy" passages I needed to get past, saying as I went in, "You know the material, Sis," and asking when I came out, "How'd you think you did?" You knew I was my own toughest judge.

A word about Grandma. Before I ever knew the word "adore," I adored Grandma. In the troubles to come, I drew strength from Grandma's faith in my intellect.

"Carla Nan knows lots of things."

And, importantly, I drew faith from her moral instruction. If I were about to do something bad, like put my shoes on the bed, she'd say, "Now, Carla Nan, you *know* that's not right," implying I carried around my own moral compass. Bless Grandma.

You were so proud of my music-making; my brothers were, too. They've both told me one of their best childhood memories was hearing my playing waft through the house. You had your favorites from my repertoire. You loved Brahms as much as I did.

It makes me glad to think Brahms made your heart sing as he did mine, especially his Opus 118, Six Piano Pieces. You told me often you wanted me to play the ballade from Opus 118 at your memorial service. But as you knew, in these last years, I've developed Dupuytren's contracture in my little fingers, a genetic gift from Dad, whose fingers became terribly cramped. Sadly, as I can't play anymore, I couldn't play at your service.

As a child of the Great Depression, you wanted me to "learn the value of a dollar," so you sent me out in the summers to pick strawberries, starting in fourth grade. I earned the money to buy my school supplies and the fabric for the clothes you'd make me. But after several summers of back-breaking work—I still have pebble marks in my knees from sliding down the rows—and as I advanced in piano, I wanted to go to music camp instead. But it was out to the fields.

You'd run the bath for me when I came home, and knowing I'd gorged myself in the patch, you'd laughingly announce, "Guess what? We're having strawberry shortcake tonight!" Verrry funny.

You insisted your kids work to earn money. We were never given an allowance. I baby-sat, gave swimming lessons, typed Dad's bills to patients (and learned medical terms like angina pectoris), and, yes, picked more strawberries.

Central to your life was the Church—Westminster Presbyterian Church. You were raised in the faith; you raised us in it, too. We all loved the building, built in the late 1800s. It had stairs leading up to the darkened sanctuary, the choir loft, the beautiful pipe organ, and especially the stained-glass windows—to the north, Christ in Gethsemane, to the south, the young Jesus in the Tabernacle.

You impressed upon me the idea of sanctity. When I was four or five, I sang, "Away in the Manger" and messed with the lyrics. "Little Lord Jesus" became "Little Tord Tesus" and you intoned against taking the Lord's name in vain. Throughout your life, in reference to the Biblical teachings, you'd say, "I so believe."

I know that belief sustained you in your struggles with Dad. Dad was not raised in the Church and was not a believer, so he stayed at home while we went to church, Sunday School, and youth fellowship. His absence took a moral tone for you. Dad, by default, was seen as a kind of pagan. You at least got Dad to join you in the church supper club, called Clipper Club, made up of other postwar couples who met in members' homes. Over time you became a pillar in the church, too, as Deacon and Elder. Your "church family" became vital to you. You shared the same pew over the years, in the back, with my Sunday School teacher, Meg, who as it happened died just months after you.

My favorite church activity was when we hosted foreign students from the University of Washington over the Thanksgiving holidays. It meant more work for you, but you connected with each and kept in touch for years afterward . . . students from Iran, Switzerland, Japan, Finland, Argentina, Greece, Indonesia, New Zealand, and Nigeria. You sent the Nigerian man money for many years after he returned to his strife-torn country. I remember the Iranian, flabbergasted that you made Thanksgiving dinner for twelve or thirteen people on your own. In Iran, his mother had servants to do the work.

The Early Years

As thanks, the students sent you lovely gifts such as scarves and jewelry. The earrings from the Iranian you wore until the end. I have them now.

All this bespeaks a certain prosperity and ease. We benefited, like many families, from the great postwar boom, in the 1950s stretching into the 1970s. The middle class rose and expanded in a way that today, when the rich get most of the riches, seems a dream. Kids got their own bedrooms, garages became double in size, the family vacation became a staple, a target date. We spent many lovely summer days with your friends who'd acquired beach houses or lake cabins on Hood Canal, Bainbridge Island, and Deep Lake, where people could "get away from it all." (I began to wonder what "it all" meant, why it was something to get away from.) Admirably, our growing prosperity was not something you flaunted. Instead, you bought savings bonds for your kids. It was Dad who'd indulge himself occasionally.

Dad was doing well. He established a busy practice, was in demand for consultation, and did lots of surgery. In those early years, he had his office downtown, above the J.C. Penney store. I loved going to visit him. Climbing the stairs to Dad's office felt like ascending Mt. Olympus. It was a small suite with a waiting room, examining room, and an office in back. I can still smell the linoleum and the rubbing alcohol.

Dad preached preventive medicine to his patients, and he followed his own counsel. He was early to healthy medical practices. He stopped smoking cigarettes before the Surgeon General's warning and switched to a pipe. He took up this new thing called "jogging." He gave credence to psychosomatic medicine, especially the destructive effects of stress on health.

His nurse-receptionist Marian stayed with him through all his years of practice. He became known as a good diagnostician. Other doctors called him with puzzling symptoms presented by a patient. He was proud he never lost a mother or a baby in delivery.

And he became known for his surgical skills, like sewing loggers' fingers back on. He once told me if he had it to do over again, he would have been a surgeon rather than a general practitioner. He loved the handiwork and delicacy of surgery. But as a general practitioner, he seemed genuinely fulfilled. Certainly in a small town with a minimal complement of doctors, he saw just about everything and was challenged. His most astounding surgical feat: He saved the logger, gravely injured in the woods—Dad said he was cut nearly in half—who later conceived the daughter who would marry his own youngest son, Ted.

As you said, I was "so in awe" of Dad and his medical skill. I was proud to walk around with a name derived from his . . . Carl. I heard the respect resonating in people's voices as they addressed Dr. Lofberg, especially on house calls. (I was his driver.) When we entered the house of a seriously ill patient, his reception was, "Oh, Doctor, you're here!" It conveyed the certainty that he could and would save the patient's life. The same respect emanated from patients as I accompanied him on his hospital rounds, where I also saw how the nurses and sisters at Catholic-run St. Helen's Hospital spoke in awe of him. It seemed, I thought, a wonderful way to be treated by the world.

We know how that worked out for me: I was a pre-med major in college for all of two weeks. Chemistry, I soon saw, was a language I would never crack, while Dad had majored in organic chemistry in college. I fainted while watching an episode of *Medic* that featured a cornea operation. When I came to—good thing I was lying down on a sofa at the time—I realized, *This can't work.* I called Dad with the news and told him I thought the humanities were more my line. Dad wished me well.

Like you, Dad became a pillar of the community. He served many years on the school board, participating in all the planning and decision-making required to build a new high school, the one his children eventually graduated from. But, always, his main focus was medicine. He kept abreast of new developments in the field by reading medical journals and attending symposia in Seattle or Portland. A quiet man, the most animated Dad ever became was when, returning from another symposium, he'd say, excitedly, "Carla Nan, do you know what they're going to cure next?" Compared to your more energetic self, Dad was, as you said, "reserved." He was not chatty. Finns, he said, spoke only when something needed to be said. He was most chatty and relaxed with his poker club, made up of other veterans of World War II; he enjoyed complaining about his "lousy hand." They played on an Army blanket spread over the table.

Who had more patience than Dad? I smile remembering this. In junior high, I accompanied Dad and his friend Bob Veneman for an overnight of camping at Spirit Lake, up at Mount St. Helens. Dad and Bob were out on the lake, fishing. I was onshore at the campfire warming a dinner you'd prepared—chicken and hash browns. But dinner got delayed because Dad lost his glasses in the lake. Since the lake was crystal-clear, he decided to fish for them, and finally after several hours, he snagged them, Bob chuckling all the while. However, Dad's patience would soon be tested.

Around the house, Dad always had some sort of reading material in hand, usually medical in nature, but also (this tickled all of us) the funnies in the newspaper. He studied them, laughing quietly and helplessly, especially at the worldly wisdom of Pogo. He also kept up on the best-sellers in literature, like *The Catcher in the Rye*. I'd picked up there was some notoriety attached to the book (I was probably in junior high by then). I read it on the sly and was stunned. Kids could mouth off like that? Around the same time, I also read Dad's copy of Norman Mailer's *The Naked and the Dead*, expecting something steamy, not a World War II novel. Dad caught me reading it, an encounter I managed to turn into a seminar.

"Dad, the enlisted men in this book really, really hate their officers. You were an officer. Were you aware of the hatred?"

Dad, who as you said was "never too aware of things," said no.

Significantly, at least for me, Dad loved listening to classical music. At a time when this thing called "rock" was starting to shake, rattle, and roll noisily, it meant something that a parent held out for thoughtfulness and beauty. On the Magnavox he'd play Tchaikovsky's ballet *Swan Lake*, which, dance for dance, seemed beauty incarnate, and Beethoven's "Sonata Pathetique," which seemed to conduct a very serious conversation with the listener. He also developed a taste for opera. He loved *La Traviata* and *La Bohème*, especially, from the latter, *Musetta's Waltz*. We'd hear him humming, which, since he could not carry a tune, was painful to hear, and we'd all roll our eyes.

When friends asked him if his daughter got her piano-playing talent from him, he'd say, "Well, I play the record player."

But his favorite composition, he said, was his daughter's. In my junior year I was asked to compose the overture to the school play *Look Homeward, Angel*, which I would perform on the piano. Since the play was set in the World War I era, I strung together a medley of tunes from the time: "Over There," "By the Light of the Silvery Moon," and "K-K-K-Katy." The only original composing I did was the bridging between tunes, but Dad thought it was Beethoven. For decades, every time I came home for a visit, he'd "request" I play it for him, he loved it so.

I see I speak of love a lot here—your love of your friends and your church, Dad's love of medicine and classical music, and my child-love of you both. Because, of course, I am writing of two deeply human, interesting, full-bodied people . . . my beloved parents. And even though you and Dad were not demonstrative toward us, and though you seldom directed at us the actual words, "I love you," we knew we were loved. We three were the sole subject of your serious, serious attention and hard,

hard work. Not all of my memories of my childhood and our relationship are of pain; there was a lot of love. The sweet in the bittersweet.

Now for the bitter in the bittersweet . . . the sad, hard part.

Though we seemed a model family in our small town, with Dad a leading professional man and you a dynamic pillar of the community, I sensed something "off." It was more a matter of omission than commission, a lack, through the years I was in second through seventh grade. I didn't want to acknowledge a "problem," because that meant a concrete threat to our existence as a family. It was more amorphous.

What was "off"? Mainly, it was the lack of talk and the lack of laughter between you and Dad. By now I had two bases of comparison. One was the new TV series, *Ozzie and Harriet*, which featured light banter and gentle laughter in the family, with the not-very-complicated problem always worked out by program's end. We watched the series together as a family, which seemed to me implicit agreement that standard family life was meant to be pleasant and placid.

The other basis of comparison I had was the home life of my classmates, the day-to-day relationship of their parents, especially in the grades before high school. I spent tons of time in my friends' homes—Karen, Lois, Claire, Annie, Dorothy, Sally, Jack, John, Brian, Steve, and Jeff.

I studied how my friends related to their mothers. Was it easygoing or more formal? Were there hugs, which I had started to miss from you? With keenest interest I noted what happened when the father of the family came home. Did he kiss his wife? Did his wife kiss him? How did he greet his kids? How did my friend relate to her/his parents? I wanted to know how other families worked. Who, as you put it, "ran the show"? Whose word was final? Was it the mother or the father? And if the mother was in charge, did that mean she had less time to give her children hugs? Even in those pre-feminist years, I saw some equality at work in the homes of my friends. Some husbands did share the power with their wives.

"You decide, honey."

By then, you clearly ran the show in our household. You dispensed; you executed. Even at the time I could see this power arrangement was logical enough. Dad was gone so much of the time with his medical practice that rather than wait to consult with him, you made the decisions. But I could see that sole possession of power didn't make you very happy.

With real heat, you'd say, "Well, guess I take care of it myself again."

Life has taught me it does no one any good to hold all the power in a relationship, because abusing that power becomes too easy, even for the most morally conscious.

But at the time, I could only observe the power imbalance in my house and ponder it. I was also aware as a kid, it was a little early to be pondering power. I had become what the author Saul Bellow called "a first-class noticer."

One thing you and Dad did talk about was medicine. Dad would mention an interesting case of his and you would ask about the symptoms. You were proud of your nursing knowledge and wanted to keep up. When you discussed a serious case of somebody you both knew, somebody Dad as a general practitioner had referred to a specialist, your voices got low as Dad told you the report.

"They opened him up, but, it was too late. The cancer was everywhere." It's how I understood early on that cancer was a killer. I also understood my parents as very smart people.

But what I missed most in our household, what I enjoyed most in others', was the laughter. By contrast, our household was a tomb. I loved hanging out at friends' houses because of the laughter and the warmth I found there. I'm not talking only of the households that spiked their eggnog at Christmas. I loved my friends' households because they were more animated. There was more relating.

Years later, when I was in graduate school in Italy—a culture that warmed me up considerably—I wrote to Dad about discovering the "light bonds" of feeling to be enjoyed between friends and family. "Which lightness," I wrote, "Mom closes down."

We found these letters in your house after your death. Dad had written to update me on the state of your marriage. Thank you for not throwing these letters out.

Even on those weekends when we joined your friends in their getaway cabins, when the whole point was fun, you and Dad didn't laugh together. I'd find you in separate groups, laughing, to be sure, but not together. An insight I had some time ago was that not even when you and Dad reconciled many years later did I ever see you two share a laugh or burst out laughing together.

I can tell you it is one of the greatest joys in life to burst into laughter with your beloved and ride that laughter out together. Maybe, after all, you didn't need it, but I found I did. Once I asked you, when I was in fifth or sixth grade, why you and Dad didn't laugh much together.

"There's more to life than yuk-yuk," you had said. Later, in high school, when I raised the question again, you said, "Oh, your generation. All it wants is to be happy."

Well, yes. I would eventually come to have all kinds of arguments with my generation, the boomers, but the expectation of happiness was not one of them.

Sensing the growing tension between you two, I tried to figure out what the cause was. I spent endless hours thinking about it, formulating the problem. *My parents, individually, are just the greatest people, but why are they not so great together?* Was it because you were turning into the disciplinarian in the family with Dad gone so much? I knew you feared becoming "the meanie." You said so many times, because you had to be "the tough guy" with us and Dad didn't. Was it because you had to attend PTA meetings and parents' nights alone? With all your activity, you had little time for yourself.

I remember you saying, often and with increasing anger, "When do I get *my* time?"

This had a profound impact on me, but also a physical toll on you. Being the perfect mother and model doctor's wife naturally tired you out. But, tired out, you could be sharp and biting. You were also beginning to see the drawbacks of being a doctor's wife.

At our rare family outings for a drive-in movie or some fine dining at the St. Helen's Hotel, invariably the message was delivered.

"Dr. Lofberg, please call the hospital."

Your exasperation was loud and clear. It morphed into fury when Dad treated himself, without consulting you, to a new car: a Volkswagen beetle. He did it again later, with a sporty Porsche.

Dad, what were you thinking?

Mom, I understand your fury. And I understand why you refused to ride in either of those vehicles . . . "that thing" . . . ever.

Finally, as fodder in my pondering, I had heard of such things as extramarital affairs, where the husband or wife cast their eye elsewhere. But, with you and Dad, I never feared that possibility . . . ever.

You, Mom, were too morally sturdy ever to indulge and Dad, though we saw him less, had eyes only for you. He idolized you. No, it was something else, but what, what, what?

In turning this problem over in my mind, I knew I was not having the normal childhood. I could feel the carefree child in me slip away, with a more careworn figure taking her place: I was actively caring for my parents' welfare, actively pulling for them to stay together, and the anxious caring was wearing me down. I could feel the foundation of our family tremble under my feet. Was I being overly dramatic? Nobody was explaining anything to me; I had to ferret out my own explanation.

Whatever the "something off" was, it grew and grew and was most vividly felt, at least by me, on our Sunday afternoon drives, the "family drive."

Oh Lord, those Sunday afternoon family drives. I shudder to think of them, the terrible tension. I can still see you in the passenger seat, looking out your window, pointing at some passing object and saying, half-heartedly, "Oh look." Dad is driving, not saying anything. We kids are in the back—I in the middle, J.C. and Ted to my sides. Around us, the tension swirls, becoming more viscous by the minute, until—I'd feel *such* a powerful urge, in my mind's eye I could see myself actually doing this: I'd lean forward and push you two together, my beloved but clearly unhappy parents, and beg you, "Please talk! You guys have s-o-o-o much to talk about!"

It was during those wretched Sunday afternoon drives, taken for the ostensible purpose of family togetherness, that I most felt our isolation from one another, that I could actually say to myself, *My parents are unhappy, my family is an unhappy one.* Later, I came to feel that an unhappy family confined in a small space and engaged in forced activity together had the explosive power approaching the thermonuclear.

And it is now, again, that I feel such sorrow for you and Dad, hurting in your isolation, and I feel the same urgency for any people hurting. "Please talk!" All of which has had profound effect on my own life with Larry.

If I was feeling the tension, I was wondering about my brothers. Being older than Ted, J.C., like me, could tell "something" was "off."

He'd ask me, "Why is Mom always angry at Dad?"

I'd tell him I didn't know exactly, but acknowledged there was a problem; he wasn't imagining things. I could tell, though, he did not feel the same need to find out exactly what the problem between you and Dad was *and* the need to do something about it, which I as the oldest child was coming to feel. I know J.C. gives credence to birth order in a family; in his eulogy to you, to lighten the proceedings, he referred to himself as the middle child, "the forgotten one."

Which touches on the quality that, I believe, saved J.C. in those early years and serves him to this day: Along with the close-knit circle of friends he has maintained from childhood, it has been his wit, his delightful sense of humor.

Over the years you voiced frustration with J.C., even some disdain. "He's always joking." You said you couldn't have a serious conversation with him. But as I explained to you during our rehab, it was you and Dad who were responsible, because one way to deal with the frightening fact that your parents are not getting along is to chase the fright away with a joke—to laugh at the scary thing.

I was never entirely sure you accepted my explanation, or even understood it, because that would've required that you acknowledge how profoundly the "troubles" between you and Dad affected your children, which you never actually did, not in so many words. J.C.'s response to the tension—to joke—was a perfectly valid response, and healthy, too. It started with puns and stayed there for a *pun*-ishingly long time (easy to see how he became a high school English teacher)—and advanced to a philosophic view that saw life as the human parade, full of faults and foibles, but fun can be had, too. Of the three of us, J.C. has always had the biggest heart, which can be wounded the deepest. Franz Kafka spoke of "the wound." For my brother, the wound began with the tension between you and Dad, and he salved the wound with wit.

I realized, even then, as an anxious preteen girl, that I was practicing family psychology without a license. But members of a family, especially a family starting to slide off the rails, will—to the best of their individual ability—grapple with their problems as they see them:

"What is he thinking?"

"Why is she angry?"

"What's going on here?"

While the boy J.C. sensed the tension in the household, enough to ask, "Why is she angry?" he also needed to keep himself away from the heat, the danger. I, on the other hand, being the oldest, really took to heart the idea of the oldest child as the "responsible one." (I give credence to birth order, too, like J.C.). I continued my reconnaissance, "walked point" so to speak, trying to figure out, "What *is* going on here?" Something threatened the family and I wanted to protect it.

The threat, as I soon understood, came from within.

That threat broke into the open, in a frightening manner—shall I call it traumatic?—when I was in seventh grade, 1957, in the fall. Dad and I had been to see the movie, *The Student Prince*, in which Mario Lanza did the singing. Dad, the opera lover, loved Lanza's tenor voice, which could do things he certainly couldn't do. When we came home, I went to bed, while Dad went downstairs to listen to more opera. As I went to sleep, strains of music filtered into my bedroom through the vent; I could hear Dad singing along . . . or try to.

All normal, except for this: You, Mom, were sleeping with me, not with Dad, and had been for some time, perhaps weeks by then. Though I didn't know anything about "the birds and the bees," even though my classmates were starting to buzz about the subject at school, I knew it was not a good sign if husband and wife were not sleeping together. But since you had been sleeping with me for a while, perhaps this was our new normal.

Suddenly, in what seemed the middle of the night, I was awakened by sounds of struggle just inches away from me. *My God, are we being attacked?* It was Dad, trying to pull you from bed! Can a twelve-year-old have a heart attack? My heart started pounding like a jackhammer; I tried to scream, but nothing came out of my mouth. In the moonlight, when I dared to look, I could see Dad pulling at your arm and you resisting. Finally, after what seemed like an eternity—I couldn't hear what you said, you both kept your voices low—you got Dad to leave.

This was not normal. Ozzie would *never* do this to Harriet. Was this divorce?

I found my voice, and I cried out to you, "Mom, what's happening to us?"

You said it was something between Dad and you and I shouldn't concern myself with it. *But how can I not concern myself when the most calamitous thing has happened just inches away from me?* I so wanted you to hold me, your daughter who, even though she'd undergone a growth spurt and reached her full adult height of five feet ten inches, was, right then, a frightened and whimpering mess; if ever I needed soothing, it was then. But you didn't. You told me to go back to sleep.

Somehow, despite my fright, and perhaps thanks to my growth spurt signaling the maturing to come, in that moment I expanded my scope—winched it open wider—from myself to include you. I suddenly understood that Mom was also hurting, though she wasn't admitting to it; I needed to help her. And in my first conscious act of magnanimity toward another person, the sign of being grown up, I stretched out my hand to you, to soothe you. But you pushed my hand away, rather roughly I thought, and told me again, "Go to sleep." I was devastated yet again, devastation upon devastation. All soothing, all warm embraces between us stopped that night. You were no longer My Explainer; you were no longer My Protector.

Decades later, during our rehab, I asked you about that night, which you could only "vaguely" recall but which I recall so vividly. (This is the way with human beings, isn't it? One remembers something vaguely, the other remembers it vividly, generally, I have found, according to their need to know or, more self-protectively, not know.) You did say you did not like that I was "getting caught" between you and Dad, thus your pushing my hand away must have been your attempt to "downplay" the tension and tamp down your daughter's fright, not acknowledge a crisis.

However it was later interpreted, with that frightening night, That Awful Shameful Night, the earth cracked open, and my childhood was sundered in half—happy childhood over, replaced by tragic sense of life. A shadow now hung over me; my heart actually felt heavier. When I learned the meaning of the German word *Weltschmerz*, "pain of the world," I instantly got it: the pain. When I looked back on my childhood, so carefree and happy, it seemed eons ago, caught in sepia tones, a fool's paradise. I could not connect that carefree happy child with . . . whatever being I was now becoming. I felt so alone, cut off from you, cut off from Dad—I didn't know what to make of a father who could behave as he had in his daughter's presence—and cut off from my younger self. If only someone had explained . . . .

Certainly, I could not share this frightening experience with my friends. I could not even see myself forming the words to describe it; and even if I could, they might be so shocked that they would shun me or find reasons to avoid me or, just as bad, pity me (I already had your gene of pride). And because I couldn't share it, I came to see our situation as shameful. Our family, a model family in the community, now bore a stigma of shame, a black mark. Back in the 1950s, the dysfunctional family and divorce were unknown, not as common as they were soon to become;

we were dysfunctional before it became a trend. The question became, "Would we get eaten up by the monster called Divorce?"

To my friends who were buzzing about the birds and the bees—love, sex, and marriage, but mostly sex—I wanted to shout, "You guys have no idea how scary all this stuff is. Stop!" In terms of my social development, the timing of That Awful Shameful Night was probably a good thing. In seventh grade I had discovered boys and acquired one boyfriend only to shed him for another. Your daughter had become tall, slender, pretty, ready. She needed slowing down and she got it, the hard way.

With time, I shared a bit of the awfulness with my friend Lois, drawn to her out of need. Lois was funny, she could crack a joke when most needed, she was daring and not too enamored of convention, also she was an indifferent student compared to my industry. I felt she might do me some good, bring some relief, loosen me up. I told her no more than, "My parents don't get along too well." Not even with the jokester could I talk about That Awful Shameful Night, because there was nothing funny about it. (Eventually I learned the saving skill of wit myself: when to apply it and, importantly, when not.)

I also made another conscious decision. I would shield my brothers from the shame of That Awful Night and from the fearful prospect of Divorce. J.C. I already saw as a tender heart who might not weather the storm, certainly not the fright of learning Dad tried to drag Mom from my bed. *Let him go be a boy*, I thought. Let him have fun, enjoy his great set of friends, develop his wit, play his baseball, build his model airplanes. And certainly Ted—Tedso, "the baby," still in elementary school—needed to be spared. Big Sister would protect Baby Brother. To this day I sometimes forget myself and introduce Ted as "my baby brother," which he accepts good-naturedly; it comes automatically from the vow I made to myself to shield him and J.C. from whatever was to come. I came to see us, my brothers and me, as a subset of the family, collectively imperiled, and I was now Our Protector.

Of course, in taking on these responsibilities—shielding my brothers, keeping our family's shameful secret to myself, not sharing with my friends, not even sharing with my beloved Grandma—I was compounding my isolation. *Is this what being grown-up means?* I wondered. If so, as I inwardly worked it out, the weight simply had to be borne, like Atlas holding up the world or Sisyphus pushing a rock up the mountain, metaphors I had learned about in my voracious reading.

As if to confirm the reality of the new weight on my shoulders, the new metaphors, our minister's wife, Mrs. Shuman, who'd also been my fourth-grade teacher and knew me fairly well, said to me, "Carla, you are *so* mature for your age."

She said it admiringly, but I wanted to say back to her, "I don't wanna be mature, not yet. Help me!"

A teeming silence became our family's normal. Not a word was said about That Awful Shameful Night ever again—not at breakfast the next morning, no word of explanation or even acknowledgement from either you or Dad about the calamitous night before, nor ever thereafter. Not until I brought it up again decades later during our rehab. I came to see our family as living on the slope of a long-slumbering volcano— you never knew when the volcano might erupt.

Living on the slope of a volcano, how does one cope? Seeing that help was not on the way and the leaden atmosphere reigning in our household was there to stay, I doubled down on all the outlets at my disposal: my studies, my extracurricular reading, my piano. People now complemented me on my "expressive" playing, but I wanted to scream, "If you only knew why my playing is so expressive. Help me!"

Another flashpoint occurred two years later. During that interim period, by far the high point for me and a welcome respite from the tension was the Van Gogh trip. You took us three out of school for the day, along with my friend Claire, and drove us down to the Portland Art Museum to see an exhibit of the paintings of Vincent Van Gogh.

Unbeknownst to me—already we were withholding our likes and dislikes from each other, things normally shared in families— you had developed a liking for Van Gogh's work. It was something about his colors, his choice of ordinary people as his subject, or it may have been the expressiveness of his brushstrokes that you, an increasingly inexpressive person, could enjoy only vicariously. You saw the notice in *The Portland Oregonian* and while culture was usually Dad's bailiwick, you decided we would have a cultural outing.

Van Gogh overwhelmed both of us. We, you and I, moved together —from painting to painting, one or the other of us exclaiming, "Oh, Mom, look at that!" or "Oh, Sis, see how he did that."

Whether it was Van Gogh's power or the power of being in sync with my mother again, I was near tears; you were happy, too. Then, for lunch, you took us across the way to a diner called (I think) The Spot; its specialty was, as paraded past our table again and again, enormous slices of green apple pie ala mode. To all our astonishment, you, who never even let us eat candy or soft drinks, announced, "We're going to skip lunch and just have dessert."

Then back to the museum for more Van Gogh. *Happiest day of my childhood, it was—thank you, Mom.* At the museum you bought a reproduction of Van Gogh's "The Potato Eaters" and had a "fancy" frame specially made for it (Dad usually did the framing). It hung in your home to the end of your days; I have it now. I also have the Van Gogh postcards and art books that I sent you over the years, which you kept. And in the assisted-living facility at the end, we worked three Van Gogh jigsaw puzzles, because you liked that we, together, built "something pretty." Oh, Mom, look at that.

With the next flashpoint, I started to take a stand—openly—against you.

It occurred when I was a freshman in high school, in the evening, again in the fall. Normally I would have been studying in my bedroom, but this night I was at the dining-room table, doing an assignment for Washington State history; I was making a map, so I needed the space. You and Dad had gone out together to, I think, another dinner with the Clipper Club.

Suddenly, I heard the garage door yanked open and the car door slammed shut. You burst through the back door, slammed it, too, threw your car keys into the drawer, kept walking through the kitchen and into the dining room. And as you walked past me, you said through tightened lips, as angry as I'd ever seen you, "That's it, I'm getting a divorce." You didn't stop to discuss it with me but kept walking, going into your bedroom, where you slammed the door again.

What was happening? Was this it? Finally, after so much tension, the end?

I waited for Dad to come home, for what seemed like hours. Again, I was reduced to a quivering mass of nerves, instant stomachache. But this time I realized, I needed to step up—do *something*—or else, gauging from your towering rage, our family would be smashed. I knew I still had an out. I could retreat into my bedroom, like a child. But I was no longer a child. Retreat would be cowardly, only a child takes the easy way out. *No, I must take responsibility, I must act.* I tried to calm myself, be ready to step up . . . but, where was Dad? You two left the house together. Then I realized, you drove home yourself and left Dad to walk his way back.

Finally, Dad arrived, quietly, through the back door. He sat down in the kitchen, in your seat at the table, not his usual seat. I readied myself for a calm presentation, a calm discussion. I got to the threshold of the kitchen, stood there. He looked so deflated, so unhappy. I said, calmly enough, "Mom says she wants a divorce."

Then, suddenly, I was sobbing, "Oh Daddy, don't leave us! Please, don't leave us!"

Dad said, a decade later, that it was my "tearful plea" that kept him in the marriage.

Again, not a word was said the next morning, just like before. You were out in the kitchen, making breakfast; Dad showed up for breakfast (after sleeping on the sofa); and life seemingly went on. "Pass the milk, please." *How's it possible,* I wondered, struck by the sheer weirdness of it all, *that calamity happens in the night, but not a word is said about it the next morning*? I also began to think, *Not only is this weird, but this is not right.* This simply is not a sustainable way for a family to function.

Of course, I was to learn many families did function this way, including my own unhappy family. But, from this point onward, one thing would be different: *I* was not going to function this way, letting important things go unaddressed. If there was a python under the carpet, how could you *not* address it? (Pythons can kill.) The important thing here was my new recognition: Dad needed defending. Even though Dad was at fault for much of your distress: not consulting you about the cars and, as I figured out later, not consulting you about his plans to build a clinic. I believe that was the cause of your fury that night you drove home alone, leaving him to walk. Now you became more outwardly antagonistic. Dad was always a slow and soft speaker, but now you went after him.

"Oh, suck it out your thumb, Carl. Say it!"

But now, I would push back. "Be nice, Mom. You're a Christian, you're supposed to be nice."

If only one of you had said to me, "This stops now. This is our problem, not yours." But neither of you did. And so we struggled on, increasingly enmeshed in our tragedy—a Greek tragedy of family conflict—and stayed enmeshed for a long, long time. Instead of diffused tension pulsing throughout the household, now the sides were clarified: father and daughter versus mother. But in the clarifying, our positions also became stultified, just about impossible to revise. We were stuck.

Yet, in that unhappy time, Mom, something important happened to your daughter. My development as a moral being was forged in that cauldron. "Was forged" actually is too passive; I actively forged a moral consciousness. By then I had learned about the Holocaust, the genocide of the Jews in World War II. The big takeaway lesson about the Holocaust, somberly conveyed in postwar culture, was that, instead of being a bystander to crimes and injustice, as too many Germans had been while Hitler pursued his evil program, one had the responsibility to speak up, stop the crimes, and stop the injustice. And there was injustice in America, too. I had seen photos of Black people lynched, hanging from trees, while white people, including kids, stood by, even laughed. How could they? Being a bystander, as I formulated the problem, actually compounded the crime, the injustice. He, or in this case I, could make it right, but doesn't? To apply that standard in my own home: Wrong was being committed and I needed to act, make it right, not stand by or keep silent.

Seeing myself as a moral actor became then (and still is now) my abiding view of myself. I wanted to be someone who could be counted on, always, to "do the right thing." Simply put, I wanted to be a good human being. I had figured out that, on one's deathbed, one wanted as few regrets as possible, and that the worst regrets were moral, bearing on right and wrong.

With all the reading I did, becoming a writer was my natural choice of vocation. But if I were to become a writer, the highest kind of writer, one who speaks with moral force, then I could not be a moral coward in the course of my own life, and then pivot.

As often happens, an author comes into one's life just when one most needs that author's message. For me it was the French existential writer and Resistance fighter Albert Camus, who wrote of taking action in an "absurd" world, who counseled against "bad faith," who epitomized the writer *engagé*. It's from Camus I learned of Sisyphus, also the idea of Resistance. All this conscience-making I forged in the space between you and Dad and me, in that No Man's Land.

Moreover, by that time, I had joined the Church. I had taken communicant's class and been received into the fellowship. The big takeaways from that class, for me, were, "Defend the weak and the meek" and "Be compassionate, be nice." I fixed on the words inscribed in the altar table, "Do this in remembrance of me," and took a vow: I will. As an added complication, our next-door neighbor, originally from Texas and also a member of our church, told inappropriate jokes about Black people at our table. Afterward, I'd ask you how you could tolerate this un-Christian behavior, "He couldn't tell those jokes in church."

Your response was, "He's our neighbor, we have to live with him."

So now, Mom, you had a crusader facing you. Instead of Defender of the Faith, I was Defender of the Father—Dad. Whenever "that tone" rose in your voice against Dad, I intoned back, "Be nice, Mom." This is not to say I was fearless . . . far from it. When you were angry, you could scare the daylights out of me; I actually quaked. When later I came across a quote by Anonymous—"Courage is fear that has said its prayers"—I remembered those times of showdown between you and me and thought, *That states it.*

Dad, seeing me step forward as his defender, now would consult me about you. This often happened while I drove him on his house calls after dinner. Invariably his first question was, "Why is she so hostile?"

"Well, Dad, buying the VW without consulting her, and now buying this Porsche without consulting her, you hurt her." In our maiden voyage with the Porsche, when I was in the driver's seat, Dad wanted me to note how smoothly the car zipped across railroad tracks. "Dad, pay attention here, we're talking about you and Mom." Unlike with you, I could speak candidly with Dad. I could bring up the big sticking point—the clinic he was building with the new doctor in town, Dr. Wayne Smith. "Mom heard Marge Smith is doing the decorating of her husband's office, but you haven't asked Mom to do your office." But Dad thought you, whom he saw as a Super-Mom long before the label became popular, were too busy with the household to be involved in his business.

Besides, as Dad rather lamely tried to justify himself, citing the cultural standard of the time, "I always thought it was the man's role to make such decisions," to which I replied, exasperatedly, "Dad . . ." I pointed out to him that the wife wants to be consulted on things like where in the country they will live ("Mom feels you just plunked her down in your home state and yanked her away from her people in Ohio"), as well as on big household purchases (like cars) and new ventures (like building a clinic).

Also, invariably, I would appeal to Dad to get the both of you to marriage counseling, something I had read about in the "Can This Marriage Be Saved?" column in *Ladies' Home Journal*. (It was this column, about marriages under strain, that instructed me about extramarital affairs, domestic abuse, and damaged kids. Our family wasn't at that extreme—not yet, not if I could help it.) Dad said he thought marriage counseling could help, but that you, Mom, were against it—on principle. People, you felt, should figure things out for themselves. They don't need counselors—a principle natural to the supremely self-reliant woman you were. When you said the same to me—it became a mantra of yours—once in a while I'd work up the nerve to say back to you, "Well, then, figure it out." As far as I could tell, you and Dad were not doing much in the way of figuring or working things out. I know you two finally saw a counselor in Portland—once—but you didn't go back, and nothing in our home changed.

You used to make fun of the whole therapeutic enterprise. You'd comically wring your hands and say, "Oh, I can't cope," then roll your eyes at one more modern thing that was "for the birds." With time I have come to think that's pretty funny, also accurate. Yes, too much of American culture has become "touchy-feely," with everyone having their "issues" and running to a therapist; best to figure things out yourself. But back then, you and Dad really did need to consult a marriage counselor, but since you didn't—or wouldn't—you had me. And in my opinion, unprofessional though on-the-scene as it was, I saw your main problem: Dad hated conflict and you were too angry to trust yourself to discuss things calmly.

Sometimes, it got a little rough, in fact quite rough. You accused me (and I use the word "accuse" advisedly) of "making things up" about you and Dad, and that—another mantra of yours: "Every marriage has its ups and downs." Pushed to the wall like that, by my own mother no less, I had to roll out exhibits A and B—That Awful Shameful Night when Dad tried to pull you from my bed and that other awful night when you were so steamed you threatened divorce and I had to beg Dad not to abandon us. "Mom, no way is all this normal."

Then, inevitably, your *coup de grace*, delivered with curled lip: "Oh, you're so-o-o sensitive." *Unjust!* That stung me to my core. I wanted to scream back at you but did not, because I could not trust myself to discuss this stinging injustice calmly. *It's because of the troubles between you and Dad—troubles making me, your own*

daughter, suffer with worry—that I am "so sensitive." You're so big on
figuring it out—figure it out, duh!

So, there we were . . . glaring at each other across the kitchen
table. And, yet, while I was trying to be brave, as brave as you,
and keep up the glare, I was crying inside. *Oh Momma, stop this*
suffering, yours and mine. Please, please, protect me." I had lost my
Explainer *and* Protector. Going to sleep, I would pray to myself,
"Jesus loves me, even if my mother doesn't."

While you and I were being driven apart—a wall of ice
seemed to form between us—Dad and I grew closer, telling each
other about ourselves. Dad told me about his mother's death, a
story you knew because you were there, but it's the kind of story
that binds people closer together. You were still in Texas with
the Army when he got word his mother was in the hospital, in
Aberdeen. Explaining to me that a Finn from the Old Country
would go to a hospital only if he/she were dying, Dad knew he
had to get to her before it was too late. You had a car but had to
ask friends for their ration cards to buy tires and gas. You drove
day and night, not stopping except for gas, sleeping while the
other one drove, with me an infant in the back seat.

Finally, when you got to Washington State, you asked Dad to
stop a while, because I was crying and needed food. Dad stopped
at a roadhouse outside Toledo, a tiny town south of the town where
you'd ultimately land, Chehalis. He went in to get me some soup,
and on his way back to the car, Dad said that, suddenly, a shudder
passed through him and he began crying. He knew. His mother
had just died. When you arrived in Aberdeen, you learned, she
had died at that moment. I asked him how he knew. He called it
"heightened awareness" and "complete certainty."

Another story Dad told me, at my request, was about his war
experience, specifically the landing on Kiska, in the Aleutians.
Going in, they expected heavy fire from the Japanese who occupied the island. They knew they had to climb up a steep incline . . .

"almost a cliff." They also knew the Japanese "typically fought to the last man." But what they didn't know was that the Japanese had already evacuated. I asked Dad if he had fear, going in, expecting to be fired at from above. He said, and this is so typical of Dad, "I was . . . concerned." He said while clawing up the cliff, one man in his unit, just feet away from him, lost his courage, pulled out his revolver, and said "Sorry, sir," and shot himself in the head.

Dad also told me that, toward the end of the war, at Brooke Army Medical Center in San Antonio, where I was born, he was part of the rehabilitation team that built prosthetics for the wounded returning from the Battle of the Bulge, "the terrible loss of limbs: arms, legs," as Dad put it. That made me so proud of my father. Now when I studied the picture book you and Dad had—*Life Goes to War*, published by *Life* magazine—I was doubly grateful my dad had been spared.

In reaction to my growing closeness with Dad, you accused me of "working it" with him, "to get your way." Yes, Dad and I did things I wanted to do, like driving while underage (fourteen) and learning stick-shift. But we did things we both wanted to do, like going to the movies. Dad and I drove to Portland to see foreign films, which I sensed, being more serious than American fare, might shed light on our tragedy. We saw *Last Year at Marienbad*, *Hiroshima, Mon Amour*, and the Ingmar Bergman films, *The Seventh Seal* and *Wild Strawberries*. Afterward, we'd go to a Chinese restaurant called Hung Far Lo, where Dad would ask me what the heck the films meant—an important nod to me as a developing sensibility, though I couldn't take inspiration from these tragic tales.

One time, coming home from Portland, Dad got a painful headache and turned the driving over to me, even though I was underage. It was nighttime and raining. "Dad," I said, "I can't see." Dad said, "Yes, driving at night is 50 percent guess-timation and driving at night in the rain is 90 percent guess-timation," but, as he lay down in the back seat, he said, "I know you can do it." Chewing my lipstick off and white-knuckled, I did. I got us home safe.

Always the opera lover, Dad took me to see *Rigoletto* and *La Boheme*. I didn't make fun of him as he tunelessly sang the arias afterward, because I understood he was seeking solace.

Mom: By keeping Dad company, I just wanted to make him less lonely, less sad, console him about the precarious state between you two, because always, always, his first question to me was, "Why is she so hostile?" His suffering gave him stomach ulcers; when he poured himself another glass of milk, I knew he was self-treating. Still, I can see how my growing companionship with Dad stoked the hostility.

In his most blatant attempt to assuage you, he gave you a mink jacket. He took me to the Frederick & Nelson department store in Seattle, the fur department, and had me model for him. He was so earnest as he asked me, "Which one do you think she will like best?" You looked beautiful in it. I remember, in particular, you dressed up in a green shantung silk sheath dress with rhinestone pin and your mink jacket. I thought you were the epitome of womanly beauty. (I now have the jacket and pin.)

While I kept Dad company, I also made sure I spent equal time with my mother and did things with you. I thought it was the responsible thing to do; it was only fair. Since it had become difficult for you and me to talk, going to the movies, where we could be together without talking, was a safe option, and we went lots. We saw *Roman Holiday* (Gregory Peck!), *An Affair to Remember* (Cary Grant!), and *Love Is a Many-Splendored Thing* (William Holden!). It didn't escape me that these were love stories. Were you reliving your own? You disliked *West Side Story* for its joking about juvenile delinquency as a "social disease" and thought *Tom Jones* and *The Sting* "too racy" (I agreed). We both were moved by *The Diary of Anne Frank*.

Family vacations were a respite from the tension, a chance to "get away from it all." (I now understood what "it all" meant). I remember one vacation which related to the movies: a week in Palm Springs, "playground of the stars." As we drove into town with Dad at the wheel, you and I spotted Gregory Peck—Gregory Peck!—walking into a toy store. We both shouted at Dad, "Stop the car!" and bolted out our doors into the store like two teenaged girls. We found the star looking at a train set as the train raced around the track; we planted ourselves opposite and gazed.

Finally, you recovered your adult self and guided me out of the store, but before we got back into the car, you said in my ear, "Gregory Peck can park his shoes under my bed anytime." *Mom?* Hours later, in a Safeway, we saw Clark Gable—Clark Gable!— in tennis whites, testing the grapefruit. It was on that trip you told me the actress Anne Baxter had seen me as a child, when I was Little Miss Chehalis of 1948 and suggested you bring me to Hollywood to be "the next Shirley Temple." I thought, *You mean, I could have had a different life?* You assured me this life of ours was better than anything Tinseltown offered.

In effect, vacations aside, our household was split in half. A standoff was in place between you and Dad, with me acting the diplomat and hand-holder. I was learning it was possible for a family to live in unrelieved tension without flying apart, though that specter always hovered. To all appearances, though, we were still the model family. We regularly made appearances, together as a family, in the community at church and school events. The family always showed up at my piano recitals. At home, there was no shouting, no histrionics, no scenes either at home or in public. My appeals to you to "Be nice" were delivered pleadingly, not angrily. Anger, though there was an abundance of it in our home, was not allowed to surface or play out.

Living like this, I was learning the difference between appearance and reality. In our case the appearance of bourgeois gentility versus the harsh reality of our home life: an ice palace on the surface and Vesuvius below. But, presenting this mask required something I learned in church was a sin—hypocrisy—acting the Christian and right thing in public but doing its opposite in private. Whenever we'd appear in public together, in what I came to see as "our family act," the thought churned inside me, *You think we're a model family? Oh boy, we're not!*

Further, it made me feel guilty and so, so sad, yet it seemed the truth: I came to see you, my own mother, as the arch-hypocrite—nice in public but mean in private to my sweet father. Our tragedy hardened further when I recalled Camus: We, the whole family, were living in "bad faith." Compounding the guilt were the illustrations of Gustave Doré in Dante's *Divine Comedy*, which I discovered in Dad's book collection, showing, in frightening detail, the suffering of hypocrites in the lowest circle of Hell.

Thus, a pilgrim's education is pieced together.

Seeing there was no relief to the tension, I worried again about my brothers. Specifically, I did not want their capacity to love and be loved, and to express love, to be warped by their parents' apparent lack of it for each other. I was worried especially about Ted. In junior high, Ted was chubby and had a lost, wide-eyed air about him. Nobody was explaining anything to him, either. When I saw him in his Cub Scout uniform with his little beanie on his head and his lost look, my heart broke for him. Applying some therapeutic psychology the only way I knew how (and providing the warm mothering we were not getting then), I'd grab Ted in a big, showy embrace and smooch his chubby face and neck.

"Oh Teddy, you are *s-o-o-o* cute!" *[mwah-mwah-mwah].* Wonder of wonders, I made him laugh! When I left for college, you'd write me that Ted "misses you so much" and tell me, "Write to him, please" (I did). When you flew him in for my college senior piano recital, I couldn't believe how tall and slim Tedso had grown. At the airport I had looked right past him.

So undemonstrative was our family that, when Dad drove me to college, after toting my stuff up three flights of stairs, as he left he pulled me to him and gave me a hug. My reaction was, "Oh God, my father has cancer and this is the last time I'll see him!"

For myself, if I doubled down earlier on my usual outlets, now—with no relief at all on the horizon—in my high school years I tripled down. Assigned in English class to read Charles Dickens' *Great Expectations*, I also read *David Copperfield* and *A Tale of Two Cities*. I read biographies, to glean how people managed their lives—Marie Curie, Charlotte Bronte, Albert Schweitzer. In addition to Dante, I also discovered in Dad's collection *Bulfinch's Mythology*, about the titanic struggles of the gods, and I began to understand our family's struggle as primal and ancient. I discovered the Russians, specifically Dostoevsky, whose extreme characters were perhaps not the best influence for a young mind in turmoil (for example, Raskolnikov in *Crime and Punishment* killing a pawnbroker).

In my piano studies, I inhaled whole suites—Schumann's Fantasiestücke, Grieg's Holberg Suite, Brahms' Opus 118: Six Piano Pieces, Bach's preludes and fugues, and Chopin's preludes and nocturnes. When no one was in the house, I'd break into *faux*-operatic singing at the piano, my anguished heart expressing itself. I was so serious . . . too serious. The Elvis and Beatles crazes passed me by; I was otherwise engaged. Bob Scott, our class comedian, found me once at the public library, reading, frown on my face. He sat down opposite me, mimicking me with an even bigger frown. We cracked up laughing and got ourselves kicked out of the library. My first juvenile hijink! Not long ago, as Bob was dying of cancer, I went to thank him for loosening me up.

Which leads me to my classmates, about whom I could write a whole other book. According me the respect and recognition that youth needs to grow, my wonderful classmates elected me to everything and then some: Girls' League president, class officer, Girl Most Likely to Succeed (the honor that still spurs me on). Perhaps because of my serious aspect, my classmates asked me to explain things to them, either personal or worldly. After a recent reunion, I sent them a group email thanking them for making me the commentator I am today. They loved hearing me play the piano and made requests. ("Do your Brahms.") In sophomore year, some seniors got the idea of running me against a junior for student body secretary; if it happened (it didn't), it'd be a first in school history. As it was, it was the first time I heard myself described as someone "with integrity." When my girlfriends delivered me home afterward, they and you expressed more upset than I (I didn't think I had a chance); you even took my hand in yours. Though I had put on weight—I was eating too many of your cookies, out of anxiety—one of the boys always asked me to be his date for the formal dances; I never missed out. In junior year you made the dress for my *Look Homeward, Angel* performance. Even at my heaviest, thanks to your design—dropped waist, flared skirt, burnt-orange wool—I felt, for my first time, womanly. In senior year, anticipating college, where first impressions would count, I asked Dad for a diet, got on it—remember the baked chicken and hard-boiled eggs?—I lost a carload of weight and became pretty again. My classmates tracked my weight loss, with weekly weigh-ins. "Yay, Carla."

In fact, if it were not for my friends and their warm love and respect, I am not sure how I would have survived my—I have to call it this—frightening childhood. Because it was so frightening, sad, and lonely, I would not care—ever—to do it over again. I could not. Looking back, I see I was so lumbered down as a developing child with emotional distress, fearing my parents would divorce. I don't know, Mom, perhaps I was clinically depressed. At the least, I was in severe distress. Thus, projecting ahead from that frightening, sad, and lonely childhood, I never could have foretold our glorious coming together, you and me, in these last seventeen years.

For now, though, closing out this period of my teens, your voice has become largely absent in this account. I did not know if you, too, were struggling to survive. You never evinced anguish or struggle; you always carried yourself proudly, though you did evince anger, no end of it. You had your friends; by now you and they had a shared history of dealing with teenage children, husbands, life. When they called, your mood brightened, Dad's darkened. What little you had to say to me was in the nature of "You're beyond me" and "I can't reach you."

Since we were at an impasse, I studied you . . . and studied and studied you. No wonder I miss you so much now. Not only were we related, passive voice, but we *related*—at least I did— active verb. I was always trying to figure you out, *What is she thinking? And why is she thinking it?*

But in my senior year, after so much anxious study—of you, of Dad, six years by then of a shaky marriage with no help in sight—I wanted out. I felt guilty about wanting out, but increasingly I wanted out. I wanted escape. Book-learning, I had found, was easy; it was life that was hard. I could not wait to get to college and start life anew.

Throughout, I was fortified by the poem "Invictus." Usually one to remember the where and when of memory—Larry calls it "Carla's videotape"—I can't remember when I first read it. But the idea of—the magnificent, thrilling idea of—"my unconquerable soul" . . . I absorbed into my bones, heart, spine. As you and I stared at each other across the kitchen table in icy and unloving silence, "my unconquerable soul" echoed in my head and helped me return the stare. And as I headed out into the world—without the advice and counsel of a caring mother, without the shield of warm mother-love—the poem's final lines played like a refrain: "I am the master of my fate, / I am the captain of my soul." Literature saves.

Another signal influence on me to note: Bull Connor siccing his police dogs on Black people, children included, in Birmingham, Alabama. I knew it then, that what I saw was evil. And I vowed, if possible, I would someday do something about it. (I did.)

One more thing—as you used to say, laughingly, in these last seventeen years when I'd call you back after hanging up, "There's always one more thing with you!" I would always say, "Of course!"

Little did I know, in those early years, that there *was* help on the horizon, that someone else did know of our family's troubles and appealed directly to you to mend things. It was your own father. In a stern one-page letter he wrote you, he addressed "the condition" in our home which he and Grandma discovered in their visit months earlier and related "its telling effect," especially on Grandma.

"Its burden has been keenly felt by your mother," Grandpa wrote. He added, "You got it direct from the doctor its cause." Turning to his own feeling—so unlike him—he wrote, "Personally my heart is bleeding for your children and Carl." Then, pointing to "the Christian teaching," he exhorted you. "Now Mildred, for the good of your children and our homes, I feel that it is now the proper time to practice this teaching."

We found this letter when we were cleaning out your house, in your dressing room, among a stack of Mother's Day cards from your children. That this letter dated 1960 was slipped into a collection of cards of more recent vintage meant only one thing: You meant your children to find it. Doing so, you acknowledged "the condition" that I, as a child becoming a young adult, experienced from the inside. That final action of yours, Mom, no doubt done as part of putting your affairs in order, was brave and honest. Thank you, thank you, thank you.

Part Two

The Wilderness
Years

How to summarize our relationship over the next forty-plus years?

I want, of course, to get to the story of our rehab—how we melted the ice between us—but I also need to sketch in the intervening years. I might say we were estranged, but to say we were estranged connotes we had a falling out, which caused a permanent state of war or a permanent state of antagonism.

Perhaps it is more accurate to say for those forty years, we were not close. Yes, Mom, I think you would agree. Every once in a while, one of us would say, off-handedly and with no particular heat or rebuttal, "If we were closer . . ."

And yet forty years of mother and daughter not being close did not mean mother and daughter were cast out into the wilderness all that time, each to wander unhappy and damaged and alone. We both have had full and interesting lives (I hope to continue mine as long as you did). You launched into a new career, while I, after college and grad school, launched into a career in civil rights and then writing. You and Dad ultimately reconciled, while I, after an awful but brief first marriage, have made a profoundly satisfying and happy second marriage, now going on forty-seven years. And we both cultivated deep and rich friendships.

And yet, no matter how rewarding my marriage or my work, whenever I prepared for my annual flight home to visit you and Dad, I had butterflies in my stomach—or as you used to say, "flutterbies." (Strange. I use the down-homey term of the mother I was not close to.) Those deep and rich friendships we cultivated, we made with other people, not with each other. Between us, there was wilderness. An Ice Age.

And yet, in the major emergencies—not necessarily in the minor ones—we were always there for each other. After my first marriage fell apart, you sent me your prayer book, the one you carried in your purse, including a note that began, "Dear Daughter" and saying you thought that the prayers "can do much good and help you at this time." And when you had uterine cancer twenty-five years ago, I drove across the country in record time, from Washington, DC, to care for you. I arrived just in time. After your radiation implant, Dad had gotten you home from the hospital, but completely inept in the kitchen, he relied on take-out food to feed you. When I got there, he was trying to fork stale rice out of a Chinese take-out box, and it splattered on the counter. "That's okay, Dad, I'm here. I can take over."

Notice the "and yet," "and yet"? We are complicated—and yet (another one!), despite all the complications, we needed each other. The love was still there, buried.

The year I left for college, you launched your career in hairdressing. Capitalizing on all those years you had cut your children's hair and your own, you saw for yourself a new path. I had no idea you were planning this move; by then we spoke only of the most rudimentary things, not of our plans or dreams. I suspect you looked down the road ahead—children leaving home, marriage not the strongest—and realized you needed to occupy yourself. (Of all the people I have known, you were absolutely the person least likely to loll around or drift aimlessly. You didn't do drift—except in your marriage.) Harking to your childhood in the Great Depression, you often said you felt guilty if you weren't working.

"I *have* to be busy." It also occurred to me that, in learning a new trade, you could support yourself if your marriage ended. As far as I knew, the marriage was barely there.

Like a true leader, you gathered allies in your new venture. You enlisted two or three other women whose children were growing out of the home and got them to sign on to attend beauty school with you. You needed a carful to make it worth the sixty-mile round trip to Olympia and back, Monday through Friday. (You did the driving.) These women were not from your circle of friends who were wives of the professional men in town. Later you told me there was "talk" among the latter—"and not the good kind of talk"—about a doctor's wife working outside the home.

But as you said, "What was I supposed to do? Sit on my duff?"

You made it clear that, while pursuing your new line of work, you did not—repeat: did not—shirk your duties as a mother. You'd prepare an oven meal in the morning and leave instructions for J.C. when to turn the oven on, so dinner was ready to be served when you got home. You made sure your household ran as smoothly as ever.

Naturally, you wondered how it would go, studying again— you had "flutterbies" yourself. But you were surprised how well you mastered the new curriculum, how your nursing background, especially the chemistry part "all came back." And you were very proud that, on the certifying exam, you got one of the highest scores in the state. You worked as a haircutter for ten years in the beauty shop down at the bus station. (Both are gone now.) You did not much enjoy working there because "Everybody stole each other's clients."

Ultimately, you wanted to be your own boss. (I'm surprised you endured ten years reporting to a boss not yourself.) I was notified after the fact that you'd turned my old bedroom into a beauty shop. I laughingly accused you of always having it in for my bedroom.

For a home economics project in high school, I had painted my walls chocolate brown and wallpapered the ceiling—a step you thought "a little artsy." (It was a nice floral pattern.) Dad initially was not pleased with the idea of customers "traipsing" through the kitchen to get to your shop, but, looking into it, you learned you needed a separate entrance. You hired a carpenter to put in a new door, and your customers came in through the garage. Dad did the rest of the remodeling—installing a sink, turning the walk-in closet into a supply room. I offered to buy you artwork for the walls, but you said, "No, thanks, I'll do it myself," and—Mom, you are amazing—you took a class in tole painting at the community college and, *voilà*, your own handiwork, some very nice still-lifes, soon hung in your shop. (I have them now.)

Your shop was a success from day one. On shop day—Tuesdays, Thursdays, Fridays—you'd open up at 8:30 a.m., and if it were winter, you'd get the space heater going for your first appointment at 9:00. (See, I told you my bedroom was the coldest in the house.) You printed up business cards—Millie's Beauty Salon: haircuts, permanents, shampoo-sets, tints, frosts. Actually, a business card was superfluous because your clientele came word of mouth—great word of mouth. (Best cuts I ever had were from you.) While one lady was under one of your two dryers, another lady was in the chair, you working on her. Family members often drove your ladies in for their appointments; they'd stay and visit. As usual for you, your clientele spanned the social spectrum— ladies from "the hill" as well as those who couldn't pay your phenomenally low prices. (You'd treat them.) Your ladies made standing appointments with you, and they kept those appointments for years, until either they died or until you hung up your scissors for good at age ninety-one.

Millie's Beauty Salon was not only a business, it was your community, your support network. The laughter emanating from your shop filled the house, made it almost vibrate. You'd greet each lady warmly—"Come in, come in!"—and you were greeted warmly in return. Your ladies would bring you their homemade gifts—cookies, jams and jellies, aprons. You were not just liked, you were loved and trusted. (Your shop was also an amazing intelligence network. Your ladies knew who in town was doing what to whom, for how long, and why, and any new intelligence, they knew the day it broke.) You often said you could tell the mood of your ladies "as soon as they walked in the door." If a lady was down, you knew a "nice 'do would do it." One lady you could not perk up was a retired teacher whose two sons both died of AIDS. You tried so hard to reach her while giving her a perm for her yearly trip to London to immerse herself in theater-going.

Of course, whenever I visited and observed the laughter in your shop, your warmth and vivacity, the lighter atmosphere, I could not help but wonder: Where were those qualities, that atmosphere, when your children were growing up? Our atmosphere was tense and heavy, and your husband was hanging in limbo. At the same time, I could see how your ladies and your shop were your sustenance and equilibrium, and I was glad for you. Because I was glad for you, I refrained from asking the "where" question; instead, I thought, *Would have been nice.* I knew I had to forge my own way forward; rehashing the past felt retrograde. I learned to "park it." Thus our struggle, the unresolved business between us, became less a daily back-and-forth thing and more atmospheric, something that hung in the air between us. Meanwhile, as I saw from your example, I needed to find my own sustenance, my own equilibrium.

Early in this new life you created for yourself, you had to absorb a terrible blow: your son J.C.'s motorcycle accident, which put him in a coma for two weeks and which you forever referred to as a "tragedy," though since he survived, we can say it was a near-tragedy. In the life history I got you to write, you go into great detail, greater than any other event in your children's lives, describing how it happened. J.C., after his second year of college, was home for the summer working a job, and he and you had just had sandwiches and a nice conversation in the back patio. He had hopped on Ted's motorcycle to return to work when a car collided with him two blocks away, leaving him lying in the street, nobody to aid him. Luckily the high school football coach, driving by, recognized him and called an ambulance. Dad and Wayne Smith came at once to the emergency room.

Acting as nurse as well as mother, you wrote, "Wayne, Carl, and I decided this was a serious head injury" and a neurosurgeon was needed. Dad and Wayne rode in the ambulance to Tacoma, while—"not trusting my driving at that time"—your neighbors drove you up. J.C. was in intensive care for two weeks; every day of those two weeks you sat vigil in his room, Ted at your side. After spending his twentieth birthday unconscious, you wrote how your son finally came around, responding to the sound of familiar voices—you and Ted talking—and how you both stood by his bedside "and cried like babies." It became family lore that, in response to your crying and laughing, J.C.'s first words coming out of his coma were, "What's so funny?" You called his recovery "a miracle" and credited God's grace. But it was such a near thing. The prayer book you gave me was the one you read constantly while your son (your note said) lay "dying." (I was in summer school at the time. Wanting to spare me, you told me about my brother's accident *after* he came out of his coma. Thank you for that, Mom.)

I will add here that, all this detail of your son's near-fatal accident notwithstanding, you noted, "I cannot relate it completely, as I feel we wipe out certain things in our memory for survival, ourselves." I note it here because in our own relationship and the rehab to come, certain things—no doubt for the sake of individual survival—would escape our memory, both yours and mine. Perhaps a bit of memory lapse is the only way to rehabilitate a damaged relationship?

Another miracle—let's make that "Miracle"—was that you and Dad reconciled. This was in the early 1970s, after about fifteen years of tension and strife, the years spanning your children's development as young adults. You never clarified how the reconciliation came about, and I didn't press for details, not like I usually press, because I was so happy it happened. *Accept it for the gift it is,* I thought. *Don't ask about the provenance.*

It was J.C., visiting me in DC during my first marriage, who told me, "Sis, I think Mom and Dad are back together again."

I happen to think your reconciliation had to do with entering middle age, as well as travel. After you and a friend visited me in grad school in Italy, your travel bug was activated. Dad, not to be left out, joined you in subsequent trips. Over the next twenty-five years, you and Dad took two dozen tours: Italy again, Spain and Portugal, France, the British Isles, Scandinavia, Hong Kong and Singapore. Travel, as I wrote you from Italy, is a unifying experience, especially your trip to Finland to visit Dad's ancestral homeland. It became family lore how visiting the pig farm where his mother grew up, you both cried as you took in the impoverishment of her childhood, and understood her quest to leave, by herself as a teenager, for America.

I also think your reconciliation came about because Dad may have finally forced the issue. All during my college years, during my visits home, Dad inevitably would take me aside and give me a lengthy debrief on the (static) state of your marriage. As far as I knew, I was his only listening post, and after many months, he needed to talk. Usually I would commiserate with him, saying I wished things were better. But during one of those debriefs, in my junior or senior year, I expressed exasperation that it was the "same old stuff" and asked him why he didn't get a divorce? His response broke my heart.

"I don't want to eat in restaurants alone."

During my year in Italy, he and I corresponded. He wrote from his office, I addressed my letters to his office. In one letter, now actively counseling divorce, I wrote, "Dad, you're such a good human being, a highly respected physician, so long-suffering, and

I cannot understand how the simple human urge for happiness hasn't thrust you out of your dead marriage and you've gone on . . . Your marriage carries on only by dint of inertia; that's not enough. Mom certainly is strong enough to carry on and has her work. Why not relocate, perhaps in Seattle, or since you took the California medical practice exam, California?" I can imagine Dad thinking that eating alone in restaurants in Seattle or California was no better, and he acted.

However, while you and Dad had reconciled, our relations, those between you and me—mother and daughter—remained chilly. For a while I entertained the hope that, with you and Dad reunited, you and I would reunite, too. But, no, it remained hard and awkward for you and me to talk; I was always relieved when Dad, my old confidante, walked into the room. Not only were you relieved to have your husband back and did not wish to share him with anyone, most especially me, but you were deeply hurt—more hurt than you ever could express—that your daughter, your own child, not only defied you, but took your husband's part against you. Which may explain why any effort at reconciliation always broke down before it started, with your angry accusation, "You always favored your father, never me!" That was profoundest hurt talking. Had I then the acuity I have now, had I addressed the deep wound in you I'd inflicted defending Dad, would you have embraced me, too? I'm not so sure you would have. You were a wily competitor; I think you might have thought, *I won,* and motored on.

I motored on, without the warm maternal love I craved. In some ways it might be said that, in my early years out in the world, I was looking to warm up this parched vessel called my life.

College for many people is a time of blossoming, but for me, it was study, study, study. Freshman year at Willamette University was lonely, because I had not been rushed to join a sorority, and

The Wilderness Years

I lived in the "losers' dorm." You had not been to college and could not educate me in Greek life, for which, Mom, I thank you. When you visited me there, second semester, I was finally being rushed because of the great grades I'd posted. Observing an exchange I had with a sorority woman—"Oh, Carla, you must come join us for buddy breakfast!"—you looked at me and said, "Oh, gag." (I laughed.)

Where next? This time, old ties did help. Taking the advice of a friend from "the hill" in Chehalis who was going to school in Washington, DC (American University), I transferred there, only to be disillusioned upon landing at what I saw was a party school. Imagining what you would advise (I didn't have to ask), I knew I *had* to make this work. Hungry for challenge, I took a transcript of my grades to the dean of the new School of International Service, asked to be let in, and was. I majored in international relations, which I supplemented with a senior piano recital, in part to vindicate the years of piano lessons you paid for. And you bucked me up when I called you in a panic before an oral presentation of a year-long senior project on European and American art and music from Impressionism to Pop art.

As before, you said, "Now, Sis, simmer down. You know the material, don't you?"

"I do."

"Then, get in there and do it."

And I did. You flew in for my graduation and were proud your daughter was cited with honors.

Not all was study, study, study. I made deep friendships with my roommates in college, Carol Anne and Sally, and in grad school, Florence. You got to know them all and warmly approved of them. From Carol Anne, I learned about goodness and kindness; from the worldly and beautiful Sally, much about how the world works (much of it not beautiful); and from Florence, my French roommate, a veneration for art and culture. These friendships have held firm and grown, yielding great richness and insights through life's various stages. Like you, I have found deep pleasure in the friendship of women. Some women, yes, are "catty" and "back-stabbing," as you said. But there is nothing so helpful as a caring woman friend gnawing on a problem with you. (There's also pleasure of extending the care in turn.) And there is nothing like laughing together with other women—at life, including the "dumb" (your term) strictures the world tries to put on women.

Still, you couldn't say I had blossomed socially, not until I got to Italy. A short stint at the Library of Congress was made shorter when I was accepted early to the master's program of Johns Hopkins School of Advanced International Studies, in Bologna. I flew home to see you and Dad, then flew direct from Seattle to Rome. As soon as I landed, I became . . . *animata*. How is it possible to fly into a foreign country and feel immediately at home? My inner opera found instant release in the Land of Opera. Italy, *che bel paese*, had the exact tonic effect I needed—of humanity, warmth, the long-sought thing called *gioa*, imparted to me by a people who, rather than slog through, make an art of living. Within weeks, I was walking down the street arm in arm with my roomate Florence, as Italian women friends do. I learned the language quickly (thanks to years of high school Latin), gesticulating like a proper Italian. I acquired an Italian boyfriend.

In my correspondence with Dad, I described the change in me, from my "former inhibited self." About my unhappy childhood I wrote, "The thing I really missed, now that I have it, are the emotions and light bonds that grow between individuals, especially the family. We couldn't be expressive because Mom would say, 'Don't be dramatic!' or 'Act your age.' The loving attitudes just couldn't grow."

Dad wrote that he was "cheered" his unhappy marriage, which he acknowledged made my childhood an unhappy one, had not "soured" me permanently. I assured Dad I retained a "Biblical concept" of my parents—"Honor thy mother and thy father."

You visiting me in Italy was fun, and something new for us. You came with a friend whose son was serving in the US Army stationed in Germany and who became our driver. We were to meet at the Bologna train station on a certain date, but as I was hustling to get ready, there was a knock at the door—it was you.

"Hi," you said. "Oh look, you're wearing the housecoat I made you. Come on, let's go!"

How did you find me? You didn't speak Italian, I lived on a side street, on the third floor, in a locked building.

We had a wonderful time, didn't we? We went up to Venice, down to Florence. To prepare for your first trip abroad, you'd read my art history textbooks from college, so in the museums you were as much docent as observer. I was thrilled! Finally, a shared interest. Caught up in the spirit, in Venice I bought you a scarf from a street vendor, which you wore to the end of your days; in Florence you bought wall sconces, which we took down when we closed your house. See, Mom, I told you "travel exhilarates." We were all having such a good time that, finally, Florence and I could reveal to you our exact mode of travel throughout Italy that year: hitchhiking.

"It's called *autostop* in Italian, Mom—"

"*What?*" Laughter filled the car. Encore, encore.

But back in the United States, I made a major misstep: my first marriage. All I saw was a handsome man with jet-black hair, and he was passionate about me. Compared to your chilly marriage, I thought that's what I wanted: passion. But, very soon, I learned passion without character or kindness was Hell. I walked out at eight months. I felt abashed at the brevity, but I considered the endlessness of your empty marriage and knew I couldn't endure that, either. Though J.C. had just told me he thought you and Dad had reunited, the wait for you was worth it, because Dad was worth it. My "betrothed" wasn't; he was a mean man. To save myself, I needed out. Enabling my escape was my Library of Congress friend, Ellie. Upset at my distress at a catch-up lunch, despite my brave front, Ellie, bless her, announced she'd get copies made of the keys both to her apartment and her car.

"If ever you need them, you are to use them."

Days later, I did. Bless you, too, Mom. While I was still caught in that awfulness, before I bolted, you sensed something wrong in my phone calls and came to visit. You did not advise me on my situation, perhaps because you could not point to your own sterling example. But you showed up, you witnessed—and you were so glad when I got free.

That shock to this system was what I needed—actually, nobody "needs" such a shock, because it destroys some people. Channeling my unconquerable soul in a way I never had before, still shuddering at my near extinction in the abyss, and desperately seeking what the Roman poet Virgil called "the upper air," I determined I *must* conceive a new way of being. Like you used to do with old clothes, Mom . . . you tore them up and made them into something completely new. For six months, I would come home from work—by then I was at the Brookings Institution, on the editorial staff—and rather than automatically turning on the TV or radio, I sat in the quiet, for hours, and pondered, *Why did I go into that marriage when I knew it was doomed from the get-go?* I now had to admit . . . I was needy. I realized about this parched vessel: My unhappy childhood gave me the perfect excuse to go looking for love in all the wrong places—but, as I saw vividly now, using that excuse was weak and dishonest and would yield me, in the long run, a mess of a life. *Stop. It. Now.* No more excuse-making for my unhappy childhood, no more victim-playing, also no more amiable sweet-pea. I had to learn to say yes and to say no. If I were to be captain of my unconquerable soul, then I needed to act the captain and hang onto my humanity while doing it. In those quiet evening hours, I visualized over and over throwing a grenade at my feet to force onto myself a new, unconquerable way of being.

I now know what people mean when they say they are "born again."

Fortunately, the timing was right. The second wave of the women's movement was underway in the early 1970s. I thought, *I will help it, and it can help me.* I'd noticed that Brookings, a liberal think tank, didn't do well by women and minorities. Soon I was helping organize the Women's Caucus and was elected to the steering committee; I was advocating. You didn't approve, though. You thought I risked becoming a troublemaker in the eyes of the institution, but acknowledged I did have prior experience as a troublemaker, referring to me defending Dad against you. But importantly, I was not put off by your disapproval. Standing up for the civil rights of others was doing the true, right, and beautiful. Finally, this parched vessel was filling up—with purpose, excitement, even feeling heroic. I became close to an older member of the caucus, Mendy, who ultimately offered to be my godmother—finally, some maternal warmth. And, like millions of other citizens, I marched against the Vietnam War.

The timing was good in another respect: I met Larry. I had started the Women's Caucus speaker series and Larry, on sabbatical to Brookings from the Navy, attended our monthly programs. Finally, at a panel on women in the military, Larry stood up to say he was about to take command of another ship, in San Diego, and if it were up to him, half his crew would be women, "because women coming into the Navy these days have higher levels of education, plus they work harder and eat less." Impressive!

Over dinner, after personal histories had been exchanged and I'd told him I still hadn't figured out what exactly to do with my life, Larry told me: "Everything you need, you have inside you." This insight moved me profoundly. Not since Grandma had I ever been reassured about my inner richness. I continued to be impressed: I could live with this attitude.

You were impressed with the very idea of Larry as captain of a ship. Now staying with you and Dad while I made the leap back to the West Coast, I was looking for a civil rights job in Seattle or Portland. But you had another idea. You told me—I still laugh at this—"Oh, go buy yourself a new nightgown and drive down and see him." *Mom?*

I went down to see Larry, and developments developed apace. The meet-the-parents scene was hilarious, becoming family lore. Larry had brought the ship up to the Puget Sound to Bangor. He suggested I bring my parents up and have dinner on the ship. You and I dressed presentably, but Dad, wanting to impress, and heretofore central casting's idea of the distinguished physician, went out and bought a leisure suit, light blue, complete with black crocodile shoes! On the drive up while I drove, we kept giving each other scare faces about the fright in the back seat. Then, when we arrived at the pier, there was Larry—in aviator jacket, collar up, leaning on the railing and smoking a cigarette, doing his best William Holden act. We giggled again. "What's with these men?"

Dinner was a disaster—chow mein on rock-hard noodles—but Larry had been busy and hadn't attended to the menu. A tour of the ship went no better. I'd forgotten to tell you not to wear a skirt on a ship, certainly not a straight skirt. Going up and down ladders, I had to get close behind or in front of you, "so no one can see." Later, Larry suggested we go to a cocktail lounge for drinks. (I could see you wondering if this were a habit.) Once there, you did the formidable mother thing. You put your purse on your lap, looked straight at Larry, and said, "Tell me, Sir, what are your intentions with my daughter?"

Larry answered, "Honorable," then added, in a nod to your formidability, "Ma'am."

Larry and I were married months later in the church in Chehalis. You knocked yourself out for our wedding. Despite the terrible July heat, you made a waffle breakfast the day of and hosted dinner that evening at Mary McCrank's restaurant. (It was the last private dinner Mary gave, but she did it as a favor to you, her long-time friend and the daughter she remembered as "a wee one.") After a honeymoon driving down the Pacific Coast, Larry and I settled in and I landed the job of Equal Opportunity Officer for the City of San Diego.

From here on, my life got *so* much better. I was underway professionally and, crucially, underway personally with Larry. I was shedding the unhappy childhood.

I loved my new job, promoting equal opportunity—specifically, moving women and minorities into nontraditional jobs like police officer, firefighter, sanitation driver. To protect "my" women in these nontraditional areas, I drafted, in the late 1970s, one of the country's first municipal policies prohibiting sexual harassment on the job. When I told you and a friend San Diego was leading the country in hiring women firefighters, your friend said, "Oh no, no, no" and I said, laughing, "Oh yes, yes, yes." (You maintained all along I should have been an English teacher and had a family.) For the EO job I received awards, was asked to run for city council, state assembly, even Congress. For a Woman of Achievement award from the Business and Professional Women's Club, I was to give a speech in Palm Springs at their convention; I asked you to fly down and join me.

"Remember when we saw Gregory Peck and Clark Gable?"

But you passed. You remained disapproving of feminism and once said you thought it was a "waste."

"Now, Mom," I said, "isn't it a 'waste' for you to cut your ladies' hair, only to have them come back two weeks later for you to do it again?" You laughed and said I had a point.

In the context of eternity, Mom, we all engage in endeavors that, ultimately, come to waste, come to naught, yet we have to acquit ourselves in our lives to fulfill our destiny, right?

Life with Larry . . . it's been a glide, a glorious one. And here I have to become more critical of you and Dad and your marriage, but these lessons flow naturally from my childhood. With Larry and me, our long marriage gets better, deeper, and more joyous, mainly because, unlike you and Dad, if a misunderstanding arises between us, usually a matter of miscommunication, we address it immediately, we don't let it fester, we don't let molehills become mountains. And we do not give each other the silent treatment, as you did Dad; we talk things out. This is the lesson, an inverse one, I learned in the back seat of our tension-packed Sunday family drives: Talk!

Another lesson I apply is the inverse of your example, Mom, and this is the harshest thing I have to say about you. (I suspect it is what you had in mind when you asked how I would write about you.) Larry is much like Dad in that he is a good and kind man, and hard-working, though Larry is far more talkative than Dad. And because Larry is good and kind, it becomes my *moral* responsibility *not* to take advantage of his goodness and kindness, not to exploit it or abuse it or take it for granted, unlike—forgive me, but it is true—the way you treated Dad.

Dad suffered under your rule. I always wondered, *How can a truly Christian person make another person suffer, and why would they wish to rule?* This was the moral point I took from your example: Don't exploit your beloved. Also share the power. Power exists in every relationship; it must be shared or there's imbalance and conflict. Yet, despite your own middling example of a marriage, you never hesitated to give me marital advice, and I never hesitated to retort, "Excuse me?"

Two things in the fifth year of our married life marked real growth. It was the year we lived in Newport, Rhode Island, when

Larry was appointed to the Strategic Studies Group at the Naval War College. The first related to the idea of strategy: What was our strategy toward life? Larry, a poor farm boy from Oregon who'd had a normal childhood, was having a brilliant career, going from one ship command to another, so he subscribed to the "Life is a banquet" school of thought. In contrast, I, with a less sunny childhood endured in a chilly household, subscribed to a melancholy, even tragic sense of life. To which Larry—bless him!—said, "Sorry, dear, I can't buy it." Life was to be enjoyed, he insisted, no matter what it threw at you. Over time, I became a happy warrior, like Larry.

The other instance related to my lifelong wish to be a writer. By Newport I was freelancing, writing articles for newspapers and magazines. When a big magazine commission was killed, I was devastated. "I can't take the rejection, I quit."

Larry got stern. "Dear, you *have* to see yourself as a four-wheel vehicle. Yes, you just got one wheel shot out, but you have three left and they're all operational. You are a writer through and through. Keep going!"

The power of encouraging words! Larry has always been in my corner—a feeling I never had before. We began referring to each other as our *compagno di vita*— companion in life.

As the years went by, you came to love Larry. You called him "Crash-Bang." In the kitchen he banged pots and pans and left a mess. You also said, warmly, "He means well." You reported to me your friends' comments on "how beautiful Carla has become"— thank you, Mom—to which I'd respond, "It's because I'm happy with Larry." I called Larry "Sweetie," and soon you were, too. You were properly impressed when Larry asked for major command and got it: the battleship *USS Iowa*. In all, he had four ship commands in his Navy career.

You joked about it.

"How can they give Crash-Bang so many ships?"

But you were proud of him. Dad, too. He wore his *Iowa* ball cap everywhere.

I know our decision not to have children hurt you greatly. You even wrote us a letter, on behalf of you and Dad, asking about our decision. In my response, I went round and round, citing Larry's long deployments at sea—three of them in our first eight years, each lasting six to eight months, one extended to ten—meaning that I, like you, would be the full-time and nonstop parent. If that responsibility made you angry, Mom, even with Dad coming home every night, what would it mean for me, who had more worldly ambitions than you and with Larry home less than Dad? It seemed a recipe for heartache, mine but also Larry's. I believe it was realistic decision-making. But you were hurt, and once you angrily said to me, "Dad and I got gypped on grandchildren." (Some would say three "grands" are sufficient.)

Because it would hurt you too much, I could not tell you my whole concept of childhood was so tainted with pain and fright that I could not imagine wanting to replicate it with a child or children of our own. If my child felt about me as I felt about you, I'd be devastated, and devastated, I could not parent as stoically as you did. Since you and I had not addressed and resolved our painful past—you constantly resisted my efforts to do so—you could not know that you were building the argument *against* our having children. My overwhelming thought was, *Why replicate tragedy?* I do wonder, though. *Should I have laid it out to you explicitly, that until you and I ironed out the past, then no grandchildren?* But that would put too much of our power in your hands. Even after we gave you the kind version of our answer, I continued for years to ponder the Baby Question, even seeing a therapist. Finally, in my last session, I drew up a list of pros and cons, and the cons won.

The therapist said she felt I was making the right decision for me. "But the world is losing a great mother," she said in parting. Her remark lingered long in my mind. Could the new and improved Carla make the leap? Finally, though, it just seemed too great a distance.

Also, as you said any number of times, "Children change a marriage." I loved my marriage to Larry and did not want it changed.

Dad was no help. During this time span when the Baby Question was still under review, I joined Dad, to spell you, for the second half of your annual timeshare on Kauai. Dad and I were having a lovely Sunday brunch at the famous Waiohai Hotel, on the veranda, a soft breeze wafting through. I was talking about The Question, and Dad said, speaking about childhood in general, "It's a happy time, childhood, don't you think?"

I was flabbergasted! I managed to say, finally, "No, Dad, my childhood was *not happy*." The thought bubble above my head said, *You and Mom soured my childhood, don't you remember?* but he seemed not to register my point, the trait of his that angered you most of all. I did have to wonder, *On what planet does my father live?* But by then he and you were reconciled again, so perhaps his thought processes had mellowed. Or as you said, Mom, perhaps it was a matter of survival of the self—his self.

My development as a writer took the zigzag course most every writer takes to find their subject, their genre. To stay the course, I had acquired the durability of that four-wheeled vehicle Larry advised. After Newport, I freelanced a few more years, with articles in the *New York Times, Washington Post, Christian Science Monitor*, and a near-acceptance of a short story at *The New Yorker*. But it was while writing a book review—and having a tough time until I put my argument with the book's author down on paper, *as dialogue*—that I discovered a new *métier*: playwriting. It was thrilling. Writing dialogue seemed a natural fit because of the years of crafting dialogue in my head with you, Mom, especially early on when I was puzzling out what was going on with you and Dad. (Doesn't everybody talk to their mother in their head?)

In a playwriting workshop I'd joined, I proposed my first play, about a woman who tries to prevent her husband from committing a crime. That idea met with a disapproving "Ooh, sounds moral"—a bias that, several decades later, put the amoral Donald Trump in the White House (but I editorialize). I joined another workshop, this one in New York, where I learned dramatic structuring. With this tool kit and studying the history of theater from the ancient Greeks to the antiheroic moderns, and immersed in theater-going, I worked on plays examining characters—notably women, whose richly-developed portrayal the Theater stints—wrestling with the big questions, often moral in nature.

When I would describe my playwriting to you, you often said, "You pick the big questions, don't you." Damn right, Mom.

Then, a very special event occurred—the test of character I had been looking for all my life. You had faced that test in the Great Depression and World War II—the test that asks, "What am I made of?" You found out. You were made of sturdy, even steely stuff. But in the postwar world, and especially once America won the Cold War with the Soviet Union, American life became increasingly soft—I called it a helium, anything-goes life—and talk of character didn't come up, or if it did, it was a joke. Still, I was yearning for such a test.

It was in the mid-1990s. I was working on my Kafka play, in which Franz Kafka the Death Force meets Katharine Hepburn the Life Force, when I was drawn to a life-and-death struggle in real life: the siege of Sarajevo, longest siege of the twentieth century. At my request, I was connected by phone to the man who was running one of the last independent radio stations in Sarajevo, in the siege's third year, when he was faltering and on the brink of madness.

Vlado said, "I *need* to talk to you."

I sounded normal and strong, exactly what he needed. Knowing I must treat his appeal as sacred, I stepped up and stayed, through the snipers and the escalation to shelling. At one point when it seemed Vlado might die, he asked me to keep talking because he couldn't anymore, and I spoke of "manufacturing" hope and our meeting someday for coffee. After he finally escaped, I also kept with him through his early rugged months as a refugee. When we finally met, in Prague, where he landed a job at Radio Free Europe, we were old comrades, we knew each other so well. Over our coffee, Vlado told me, as he still does, that I was his guardian angel.

As arduous as that experience was, the real struggle came when I turned our dialogues into a play. Theaters embraced my script as "something of value," but then, to develop it to its "true" essence, I heard things like, "This is Mother Teresa meets St. Francis of Assisi, can they not flirt with each other?" (I was reminded the "hot" novel at the time was about phone sex.) Or "Larry must be ticked about Vlado; make Larry the jealous husband." (Larry was thrilled I had found my "proper subject," Sarajevo.) What I thought of as sacred was threatened with cheesification; I resisted. Finally, I took all those "suggestions" and put them in the mouth of Mr. Producer, a figure representing a degraded American culture. Somehow, I got three productions, including the Festival of Emerging American Theatre and Washington's Studio Theatre. I also got a clear sense my own country was in trouble—from within.

I wanted you to fly in for the play's premiere in Chicago at Victory Gardens Theater. You deputized Ted to come instead. On opening night I called you. It would have been nice if you were excited for me, but since you were more agitated about the woman Ted was seeing at the time, your opening-night comment to me was, "Is *she* there?" Huh? I was pleased that *The Wall Street*

Journal gave the production a good review and likened me to Harriet Beecher Stowe, author of *Uncle Tom's Cabin*.

Throughout these years of wilderness, on at least a dozen occasions, I tried to initiate a reconciliation between us. But we always broke down, early and fast.

You would push me away, saying, heatedly, "You *always* favored your father, never me!" and I always returned fire, "Because you attacked him, Mom! What was I supposed to do? Stand by?"

There must be some law in physics that describes us in those exchanges: two forces speeding toward each other, crashing, with the crash sending us back in the direction we came from at an even faster speed. Then the laws of bourgeois gentility would kick in, whereby, after steering clear of each other for a few hours, we would carry on, with chitchat and make-work, avoiding any mention at all of the recent galvanic crash. Once, though, after an especially sharp crash, I came after you into your dressing room and demanded, "Really, Mom, *did* you expect me to just stand by while you attacked Dad? Because that would make me morally defective. Would my mother *really* want me to be morally defective? *Really?*" You did not respond and angrily waved me off.

Otherwise, our relationship was pleasant enough, restricted to visits and travel together. Travel not only expanded, but distracted from interpersonal concerns. Whenever you and Dad visited, I'd draw up an itinerary, and you and Dad fell readily in line. When you visited us in Newport, we "did" Boston—you loved the winding streets, Faneuil Hall, and the Indian pudding at historic Durgin Park restaurant. An extra special outing was taking you and Dad to see the "Van Gogh in Arles" exhibit in New York City at the Metropolitan Museum of Art. In your many visits to us in

Washington, DC, we did the historic sights of the mid-Atlantic region—the Civil War battlefields of Gettysburg, Manassas, Fredericksburg; the seaports of Charleston and Savannah; Colonial Williamsburg; Valley Forge; and in Pennsylvania, the Amish country around Lancaster and the antique shops of Buck's County. In Washington, DC, "so full of history," as you said, we toured the White House, Capitol, Supreme Court, Library of Congress, National Cathedral, Lincoln Memorial, and George Washington's home at Mount Vernon. We went several times to my favorite building in DC, the National Gallery of Art. At the Phillips Collection, just blocks from our apartment, you warmed to the art of Francois Vuillard—his quiet interiors and patterns; I later gave you a book on Vuillard. We drove through Arlington Cemetery, saw the eternal flame commemorating John F. Kennedy, drove around the Iwo Jima memorial, and walked through the Vietnam War Memorial, a site Larry and I visited often on evening walks.

And of course, the people. I introduced you to Ellie, the friend who enabled my escape from a bad marriage. When you tried to thank her, Ellie laughed it aside, "It's old history." I had some trepidation about introducing you to my godmother, Mendy—How would you share the mantle?—but you took to each other instantly.

You jumped right in. "I've heard so much about you."

Mendy responded in kind. "I've heard so much about *you*." The laughter erupted. The photo I took of you two, on the sofa, leaning into each other, mouths and hands animated—it's priceless.

How sad to know all three of you—Ellie, Mendy, you—are gone now. Ellie and Mendy both died just months before you. The losses pile up, the memories . . .

When Dad began to fail in his early 80s with Parkinson's, you valiantly cared for him. All in the family feel this was your finest hour, which hour lasted four years. You brought your skills as a nurse, also your wifely love to the task; Dad was so grateful. I was grateful in hindsight that you had organized an eightieth birthday dinner for Dad. It was the last good time for him, pain-free. The life history I taped of you two and assembled, with photos, I presented to Dad; you said he returned to it again and again as he declined.

How you managed those years—the work, the exhaustion, the courage—we all still marvel. You added further notes to the life history I presented you, which notes we came across cleaning out your house. You wrote after Dad's death:

"The last four years I knew Carl was slowly dying, but still you think you can keep him going." You also wrote, "Carl was confined to home, church, and community. He knew he was slowing down, but he was such a good patient. I tried to make him as comfortable as possible. We had many pleasant memories of family, friends, and travel. So no regrets."

On this journey with Dad, you reported to me the mileposts—the last time Dad played golf, the last trip you two took together (which was a disaster for Dad's back), and the last time he drove a car. (I happened to be there to help you take away the keys.) The once-tall man, now terribly bent, leaned on you. You took him out for drives and to visit friends. You would not hear of hiring nursing help in the home; you were determined to nurse Dad to the end yourself. You were heroic in that.

It is painful now to recall that, at the midpoint of your ordeal with Dad, you and I had our falling-out, or rather, you unloaded on me, royally. We were visiting you and Dad, with the intent of helping you, especially in the kitchen.

I thought I'd treat you to lunch out. But as soon as we were seated, you started in on me, that I was an "unloving daughter" who had it "so easy." I recognized this as caretaker stress.

"Mom, don't do this, please, you're overstressed."

But you roared past, warming to your theme of the unloving daughter who had it so easy. Before I lapsed into shocked silence, I managed to return a few shots. "My childhood was *not* easy but *hellish*, but you won't acknowledge it" and "You'd have had it easier if you'd treated Dad nicer." Once again—again!—I heard, "You always favored your father, never me." But this time, I couldn't engage with the old rejoinder, "Because you attacked him!" This time, I felt our boat hit a sandbar and come to a jangling halt. You looked at me with purest hatred—and I got clarity, I could see *so* clearly: We were *never* going to get to harmony, you and I—*never.* You were choosing to play the martyr, take the easy way out. Yes, caretaker stress no doubt prompted your outburst, but you might have gone off on, say, your typical day caring for Dad. But no, your target was me, still me. Of course, even in this public evisceration, the bourgeois niceties applied—two well-dressed women in quiet conversation at a back table, no raised voices, no stomping off. I cut the lunch short. "Check, please?"

I was done . . . not just with lunch, but with you. *Done.* Despite some good times shared by the four of us, between you and me it was the same-old, same-old, no advance, none. (Actually, the "unloving daughter" part was new.) I have a long, long fuse, but when it breaks, it sunders. When we got back to your house, Ted was there, but Larry was out. Ted saw my ashen face and knew something was wrong. He took me out for a long walk, his arm around my shoulder, listening quietly as I gasped out the story. I told him I was "done, done, done" with Mom; he offered no appeal.

When I told Larry, we agreed we would leave immediately. Before driving off the next morning, Larry stepped back into the house and, nicely of course, told you and Dad it would be "a long while" before you saw us again. Larry said you had no reaction.

I had a reaction two days later. Driving across Canada, somewhere in Alberta, we got caught in the soupiest fog, late at night.

Larry was driving, I was navigator, straining to spot an exit. Semi-trucks who knew the road roared past us, shaking the car hard. After a half-dozen terrifying shakes, I cried out, "Any mother whose child is out here on this road tonight would weep!" Then, it landed on me: *My* mother would *not* weep for me. She might even be relieved if I were to be kill—

I stopped myself from completing the awful thought. I held it in until we were safe again in a motel, then I broke down sobbing. "My mother doesn't give a damn about me!" Poor Larry.

When we got home to DC, I stopped my regular Sunday evening calls to you. Months went by. Finally, you called me, but with no apology or explanation. Thus, the state of our relations, the nadir. You continued your trek with Dad. And I went my way. *Free at last, free at last, thank God a-mighty, I am free at last!* I was "done, done, done" with my punishing mother.

Our Greek tragedy had reached its crisis point. How, oh how would it climax?

Part Three

The Main Event

When I said I was "done" with you, I was . . . for many months.

However, we are never done with our parents, and our parents are never done with us, their children. A way *must* be found.

As your own mother, Grandma, used to say, "The only way out is through."

And we did find the way. Today is the first anniversary of your death, January 22, which gives me another opportunity to say how grateful I am that we did.

Dad's steady decline brought me home again after a year. I could see you getting more and more tired with the endless slog, but you were doing it gallantly—more gallantly than before. There was no more unloading on your beloveds.

After another year, however, you called to say you had, finally, put Dad in an assisted-living facility. You sounded so defeated, Mom. You had vowed to yourself to keep him at home until the end, but you could not keep your vow. You had finally reached your physical limit. One morning you simply could not get out of bed, you were so exhausted. Your doctor's response?

"I wondered when you would get here."

You asked me to come out, as Dad's time was getting short— the doctor said six months. What a shock that Dad died one month to the day after you placed him in assisted living, which only added to your guilt. I did my best to comfort you. Mom, you did everything humanly possible, up to the point of jeopardizing your own health, to keep Dad going.

One of the hardest things about seeing your parents grow old is to see their physical withering. When I saw Dad, in what turned out to be my last two weeks with him, he was barely recognizable. He was, as you said, "skin and bone." About a week before he died, he had stopped eating. I made a protein shake and brought it with me and urged him to eat.

"Dad," I said, "you're a doctor, you know what happens to the body when it doesn't get nourishment."

He nodded, so sweetly. "Uh-huh."

"So, will you drink this?"

"Uh-huh," he said, and sipped on the straw. After a few sips, he looked at me and said, in his endearingly slow and deliberate way, "I wonder what is to come."

Rather than buck him up as anybody wants to buck up a beloved when they express fear, I said, "Oh Dad, I know what you mean, I know."

Several days later when J.C. and I visited him, he was in a delirium, moaning. Out at the car I began to cry and asked my brother, "Is it a sin to ask God to take him?" and my brother said, "No, Sis, it is not." Dad died later that night, early in the a.m., April 5, 1999.

You woke me in the morning, early, and said, "Dad's gone." You asked if I wanted to accompany you to see Dad one last time; I said, "Not really." (Later I felt badly about that decision and reformed when you died.) I said a prayer for Dad, then joined you in your dressing-room. You were animated in a way I'd never seen before.

While getting ready, you repeated, over and over, "Oh Carl, you were my one true love, my one true love. What will I do without you, what will I do without you?"

I got worried. Could you drive safely the several miles to the facility? As you left the house, I told you to talk out loud to yourself in the car and keep your eyes on the road.

Since we all thought Dad had more time, I hadn't brought my computer with me to write a eulogy, so I used a computer at the church. While I was working there on a draft, Ted found me and insisted I come with him "right now." Your outdoorsman of a son needed a proper suit for his father's memorial service, and I was his shopper.

The service went beautifully; the church was packed, as it was for you. In my eulogy, I talked of my admiration for Dad and all his fine qualities. "How wonderful it is to look up to one's father, and not just because he was tall." You thought I got "mushy," but I wrote from the heart.

It is wonderful to write from love.

As I drove to the Portland airport for my return to DC, you sat in the passenger seat not talking much. I felt the need—the absolute imperative—to turn a corner in our relationship, otherwise how could we go on? Already the warmth of Dad's memorial service was waning. Unless a radical change was made, *now*, we would revert to our default condition—icy. As the airport tower loomed into view, I grabbed for an ice pick; I threw the switch from head to heart.

"Mom," I said, the words coming slowly, carefully, "don't you think . . . that *all* those years of conflict between us . . . were really about Dad?"

Your response was likewise long in coming. Finally, in a firm voice that betrayed the years of hurt and not looking over at me but gazing straight ahead, you said, "Yes, and I think he rather enjoyed it."

Wow! Was this the end of the Ice Age?

This was truth. This was our first "ultraviolet moment."

I can't describe this kind of moment better than I did the

one time I wrote about us earlier in *The Huffington Post* (which you liked, saying it was thoughtful and accurate). An ultraviolet moment—as you and I came to define it by our own hard-won actions—is a moment when "the world halts on its axis, the lights bump up to surgical brightness, masks are dropped, words fulfill their precise meaning, and truth comes out."

Referring to your remark—your crack?—about Dad enjoying the conflict, I wrote, "And crucially, refreshingly, this was new, this was *advance*. Granted, it entailed speaking, if not ill, then analytically of the dead. But it also signaled less defensiveness and a greater ease between us." I will add there was a marionette quality about those moments. I felt as if I were dangling in air, while the weighty business—truth telling—was being transacted.

Saying goodbye at curbside, you got the warmest hug you had ever gotten from me. We were laughing—another first for us—not hysterically, just warm laughter. I was flying before the plane left the ground.

A thought: *Could my mother and I actually reconcile? Could we actually do that?*

Another thought: *Maybe the king had to leave the stage before the queen and the daughter could do the reconciling?*

That was 1999. My next visit was only months later, in the fall. We both missed Dad so much; some days I didn't know how I could get through the day. When I told you that you said, "Me, too."

The theme here was loneliness, which led to another of our ultraviolet moments.

We were talking more generally, not just about the aftermath of Dad's death, but touching on our entire history as a family. It was actually you, Mom—you who never talked about feelings and were so stoic—who indicated your feeling of loneliness during our early years of standoff, when I stepped forward to defend Dad and told you to be nice. I heard the new note in your words and reacted.

"*You* were lonely, Mom? But, I was lonely, too!"

That was truth, another one, which I had never acknowledged out loud before, only inwardly. I had never told you, my nemesis, how lonely I had been as Dad's teenaged defender.

More truth followed when you said, "Yes. I saw you and your father as a team, and I was on the outs. I was lonely." You told me not only did you see Dad and me as a team, you saw our team as having "all the smarts," too. Not only were you outnumbered, you felt ill-equipped for our particular battle.

"Mom," I said, "that is *such* an important insight . . . insight into you, insight into me. This is *so* interesting."

We also noted Dad was probably lonely, too. Since the lines were open—at last!—I chanced another question, which led to another ultraviolet moment, ultraviolet truth.

"Mom, something has preyed on my mind for a long, long time. Did you see me as . . . well . . . evil? Because the way you glared at me, I thought you did."

"No, never," you said. You added you didn't feel much love in my glare, either.

I went on to confess—confession!—that, sometimes, when I thought of Dad's sad face, "I did think of you, Mom, as . . . not nice." In the past, which seemed to be fast receding, I *had* thought of you as evil, now and then, but that firecracker word could have derailed the *rapprochement* underway. To maintain the delicate balance, I added that you probably thought I was "not nice" at times, too. You nodded.

I think I thanked you then, which may have sounded awkward, but I was feeling awkward—I was on new terrain, you were on new terrain, I didn't want to put a foot down wrong, and you, for the first time in our history together, were cooperating, or you at least seemed open to the idea of excavating our past and rebuilding. Hope springs.

"We did good work today, Mom. Whew." I had to go lie down; so did you.

Larry and I spent the summers of 2000 and 2001 with you. You welcomed the company—you said the house felt empty without Dad—and we welcomed being away from the DC humidity and appreciated your basement's coolth. Of course, I not only welcomed the chance to advance our warmer relationship, but I also wanted to see how far we could take it. I was also simply *enjoying* my warmer relationship with my mother. After our eon-long Ice Age, what a pleasure.

I wrote another play in your basement, this one about a woman's inner life—funny, now I see the parallel—much was going on in your daughter's inner life just then. In summer 2000, my Kafka play was given a reading at the Oregon Shakespeare Festival (they'd done the same for the Sarajevo play), and in summer 2001, the Kafka play was selected for the Edward Albee conference in Alaska. Larry and I drove up.

Larry and I had started discussing the possibility of moving back out to the Pacific Northwest, and we began including you in those discussions. We took you with us as we started to check out the real estate market and look at houses for sale in the south Puget Sound area. As we walked through a house, flyer in hand, I kept exclaiming to Larry, "Dear, we could get twice the space for half the price of our place in DC."

You were encouraging. "Well, I think you two should think about it."

In spring 2001, in New York, I had seen *Mnemonic*, the play teleporting the audience member back to age four or five, standing in a field, with one's mother and father on each side. What if . . .?

But then, a glitch would occur, like the silent treatment you imposed on us the second summer that lasted several days. I can't remember the reason for the silent treatment—you took offense at something we said (the videotape has a gap here)—but with it came the old tensions, the old nausea. It got to Larry, too. Finally, after another silent dinner, Larry, whose fuse was even longer than mine, banged the table.

"Mom, you can't treat people like this!"

You left the kitchen and went to bed. Next morning, Larry was waiting in the kitchen, intent on making peace and apologizing for his outburst. While you were pouring out your Cheerios, he went over to you and put his arm around your shoulder. You said something quite remarkable for you.

"Oh, Larry, I just can't talk like you and Carla can," and you laid your head on his shoulder.

Later, when Larry had told me what transpired, as I was leaving the house for a medical appointment, you came after me. I could tell you had something to say and were anxious about it. In the old days, you stood your ground and I had to come to you, but now, you came to me.

You blurted it out: "Sissie, don't give up on me."

It makes me weep now, Mom. You were *really* stretching yourself, stretching into new territory for you—you did not want to lose us, you did not want to lose me. I gave you a quick hug and said, "Mom, of course I'd never give up on you."

You also said as I was hurriedly getting into the car since I was going to be late, "I think you're giving me more chances than I deserve."

Astonishing! In just hours, you had learned a new language, the one Larry and I used, language expressing wants and needs, sounding like nothing at all of your earlier self. Really astonishing, Mom.

Still, such glitches gave me pause about returning to your orbit. There were many good, defensible, bred-in-the-bone reasons why I had put 3,000 miles between you and me for so long. I needed the distance to feel free, to be myself. Which is *not*, as you often said, a selfish thing to want ("me, me, me"); it's what we are put on this earth to do . . . develop our *selves* so we can contribute to humanity. Could this self of mine still flourish in proximity to the figure who'd caused it so much pain and who'd not wanted to talk it out? Now you seemed willing to talk things out, so maybe? Of course, this self of mine was not the same self as in childhood; I'd be coming in with many more tools, experience, plus I'd acquired some of your flintiness, so maybe? But for reconciliation to take place, it *had* to entail addressing all the old conflict, the python under the carpet—oh Lord. I'd shudder with the old dread.

If I was overthinking it, it was because I feared having my flame, if not extinguished, then constantly having to fight to protect it vis-à-vis an all-powerful mother. I did not want to be on the back foot with you, having constantly to defend myself, not in the second half of my life. These apprehensions I churned through with Larry and also with my old childhood friend Lois, whom I may have worn out.

Finally, it was this that decided me: the recognition that if there is conflict between primal figures such as parent and child—the classic, mythic conflict—as long as that conflict remains unresolved, it skews in profound ways everything else in those lives.

It is a thing now to "offload" a "toxic" relationship but how to offload a primal one? For so long you'd played the martyr; for so long I feigned indifference—"I don't care, I don't care"—but I cared, primally. Now you showed you cared, too. You'd put down the martyr's mask and asked me not to give up on you. I assured you I wouldn't. This put us on a new path, an upward path; there was a glimmer of hope . . . let's go with the glimmer. Besides, I really liked the idea, the grand and exciting idea, of turning tragedy into—what exactly?—anything but tragedy, anything but submit to a fate ordained by the ancient Greeks. I was damned if I'd leave us dangling lamely in the crossed lines of our struggle. I began to hope you'd work with me on the untangling.

There was another consideration: Among my feminist friends—women who were making a place for themselves in the world—there was almost always the comment on their part, "I don't want to live my mother's life." Some said it sympathetically, but some said it scornfully. With the latter, I thought, *How fair is that, especially if the mother devoted her life to family? Did these women understand the context of their mother's life, the forces she had to deal with that made her life so unedifying to her daughter?* (I always thought feminism meant giving the woman, especially your own mother, the benefit of the doubt.) I was never scornful. I always admired how you navigated the challenges of your life with such dignity, but I also realized we could not become closer until our lives became less alien to each other, until we both understood the forces in our lives and, crucially, the forces at play in this struggle of ours. To reconcile, we had to come into a better alignment. I became willing to try.

By end of summer 2001, it was decided that we'd move back home, to be around you and Larry's family in Oregon. As a writer, I was portable. So was Larry. By then he had closed out a thirty-two-year career in the Navy and was consulting for UNESCO, doing conflict-prevention work (for which he has a knack, as shown in his kitchen diplomacy with you). We drove back across the country to DC, intent on selling our condo and packing up. We arrived back in the city September 10.

September 11, 2001: the day the world crashed into America, with the terrorist attacks on New York and Washington. Having arrived home late the night before, we were sleeping in, unaware

101

how history had erupted. It was my Finnish cousin's wife Ursula, calling from Helsinki, who woke us up.

"Are you all right? Are you all right?"

They had visited us and knew we lived in town. Ursula told us the Twin Towers in New York had been attacked and now the Pentagon. I jumped out of bed and ran to our kitchen window. What a horrific sight, just miles away and yet so close: the impregnable Pentagon on fire, filling the sky with a roiling cloud of black smoke.

In cataclysms like 9/11, one gets clarity—what's important in life, what's not. In that moment, staring at the black cloud above the Pentagon, I knew America was forever changed. I also knew, for myself, I did not want to continue as a playwright, dramatizing how fearful we all felt that day and thereafter. Instead, I wanted to make sense of whatever was coming at this changed America . . . thus, I'd shift to commentary. In commentary I would be able to make the moral point, which in today's anything-goes theater isn't much welcomed. The rightness and wrongness of things in America were about to be parsed; I wanted to help parse, be at the barricades.

Also in such a cataclysmic moment, it becomes more imperative than ever to get one's primal relationships right. You and I, Mom, became top priority.

We pulled up stakes in one Washington and drove to the other in an enormous U-Haul truck. Midway, Larry was phoned with a job offer as chief of staff of the newly created Department of Homeland Security. I told him we could go back; he gestured straight ahead. I learned New York Theatre Workshop would do a special reading of my Sarajevo play. In the aftermath of 9/11, at a theater near Ground Zero, my play about the saving power of human contact in Chaos would be performed. This new mode of living would work fine. As we pulled into your street, you fairly danced with joy.

"Now I have all my chicks around me," which I confess gave me a sinking spell. But soon enough Larry and I settled in and resumed our lives, the first year in Olympia, thirty miles up the road from you, then Gig Harbor, twice as far away. We fell in love with the area.

To get underway with the commentary career, I reconnected with *The Christian Science Monitor*, where I had published an op-ed years earlier on the aftermath of the Vietnam War. I came to them now with a proposal: In the aftermath of 9/11, when the call came from all sides that we needed to "return to normal," I noted America had left that station—normalcy—a decade earlier when, after winning the Cold War, we indulged ourselves in all ways during the go-go '90s. My proposal was a column titled "Reinventing 'Normalcy,'" which, embryonically, incorporated all the elements of my eventual beat: politics, culture, and ethical-moral issues. As I told you a number of times, I love writing commentary—it makes me feel necessary.

Now back to the top priority: you and me.

You seemed to accept that, in moving back into your orbit, you and I would have to, at long last, address the python under the carpet. I say "seem," because I never put that as an ultimatum, since I did not want to elicit your usual door-closing response. I was just hoping that, as two adults, face to face, we could find a way. Since you did not believe in counseling, we had to do it ourselves.

But how? How to unpack the old conflict? How to handle the old pain and get to peace? Knowing you—after all, I *had* studied you my whole life—I knew you would not stand for "the third degree." You would not tolerate being interrogated, put on the witness stand, and grilled like a criminal. Nor did I have any desire to take the hard-nosed approach. Knowing I had been involved in theater, you might have been prepared for dramatic shouting and a showdown, but I didn't want that, either. I knew any approach casting you and me as archrivals would not work, not with our family history of avoidance and muffled response. Besides, we'd been cast that way—as archrivals—forever and it had illuminated nothing but blind, bad feeling. No, indirection was key. I had to be subtle. As my favorite poet Emily Dickinson put it, I had to come at it "slant." Or as you'd say, "sly."

I also brought my own terms and conditions to the table. In my quest to recover my mother's warm love and trust, I would not beg, abase, or supplicate myself by baldly asking for the prize I sought, begging for what I deserved. I never had begged to date, and I never would now. I am proud, like you. Nor would I allow myself to be treated as the daughter whose power was subordinate to the parent's. When I said perhaps the king had to leave the stage before the queen and daughter could reconcile, I amend that to say we had two queens here, both wearing their tiaras and both wielding their full measure of power. Diplomacy was required—mutual respect between equals, peers. I decided I would keep these terms and conditions to myself. Subtle. I would roll them out only if forced.

All this was a lot to load onto the table. Again, how to proceed?

Quite by accident, I discovered the perfect approach. It had been hiding in plain sight: double solitaire. You always had playing cards on your kitchen table; on your own, you played single solitaire, "to keep the brain cells working."

In the early months of our rehab—a term I never used with you: more subtlety—whenever Larry and I came down to spend the evening with you, after dinner you would always suggest we play a few games before the long drive home. "How about some double sol?" Perhaps you were nervous about the questioning you knew was imminent; perhaps you thought a little diversion was in order. But because you threw yourself into the game—you were so competitive, you *had* to win—diversion became the mechanism of illumination.

That's how it came to light that you and I agreed on the significance of our "project." It was over double sol, early on, that I said, "You know, Mom, this mother-daughter thing between us is *the* main event," and you replied, "You betcha."

Another time, early on, I was poking around in ultrasafe territory, asking for more about how you and Dad first met. I reiterated the family lore about Dad being "pleasantly surprised" the "more beautiful gal" was meant for him and about your first impression of Dad. You thought he was "sincere, not like the 'hoity-toity' doctors" you worked with.

You picked up on that, saying you never thought you could "go for" a doctor, not as husband material. At that point in our game, you were slapping cards down as fast as you could, preparing to go out. But you were also going on and on about "hoity-toity" doctors, so I chanced a little fun.

"So, Mom, what was your *second* impression of Dad?"

First you went out—you had to get your win. Then you said, "I could see"—you actually giggled!—"he needed help."

I laughed so hard, I practically slid off my chair. You were laughing hard, too; I could tell you were enjoying being a bit naughty, telling on Dad. What joy: belly-laughing with my mother—a first! Larry came in from the front room.

"What's going on?"

Yes, double sol would work just fine.

In our next session—*er*, game of double sol—I wanted to ask why the conflict had to happen at all? Why could not one of you—my mother or my father—have stopped it at any point, preferably at the start, and nipped it in the bud? Which, in asking why, got us to the essence.

We had started a new game. I was—literally and figuratively—laying out my cards, building the seven piles to start,
when I said, as evenly as I could, "You know, Mom. All those
years of troubles between us—they could have been avoided if
Dad had said to me, 'Daughter, this is between your mother and
me. We will take care of it, and you go have a childhood.'"

Your response was explosive. "Yes!" You threw down your
cards, slapped the table with both hands, leapt to your feet, and
leaned across the table at me.

"Couldn't you see you were being used?"

Larry, in the front room, muted the TV. You and I were in
another ultraviolet moment, a big one. I remained seated, keeping
my voice as even as I could. I remember my exact words.

"Mom, I was a child, I was a kid. You were the adults." I
decided not to stress it about being the adults, the adults able to
stop their child from being used. "I guess you and Dad thought
your smart daughter was a little Dr. Freud, able to understand.
Mom, I was so bewildered, so frightened at the scary things
going on, I was way out of my depth. I saw the two giants in my
life—my mother and my father who were my sun, moon, stars,
and earth, whom I loved with all my heart—not getting along
and not talking, and you were attacking him."

Bless you, Mom, you were taking in this new information,
and you were taking it well. I saw it registering in your eyes. You
sat down again, scooting your chair in.

I asked, "May I go on?" You nodded.

You listened hard. I described the context. By seventh, eighth,
and ninth grade I had joined the church and I had learned about
the Holocaust, so I knew if a situation went wrong, bystanders
had a moral responsibility to try to stop the wrong. Bystanders
who just stood by sacrificed their soul. I said these exact words:
"I saw a wrong being done in my home, so I *had* to step in or lose
my soul." You, my mother, would have been the natural one to

advise me, but—this is our tragedy—you could not, because now you were my adversary. I also said these exact words: "It was the right thing to do, Mom, defending Dad, against you. I could not stand by. But I paid a terrible, terrible price. I lost my mother, for a long, long time . . ."

The tears came for me; they did for you, too. Not sobbing, just tears down our cheeks.

I could have gone on about how lonely and isolated I felt as The Child Who Knew Too Much. But we had already established, in an earlier ultraviolet truth, that our struggle had made you lonely, too. I harked back to that.

"It was pretty lonely for both of us, wasn't it." It was a statement, not a question.

You nodded a long nod.

By now I was feeling relief. I had said the many things I had rehearsed decades to say to my mother but couldn't—and now I had, *and I was heard. By my mother.* I could have exulted with an aria, but we were not done.

Now it was your turn, the ball was now in your court. But you didn't seem to know what to do with it. In this longest, most important ultraviolet moment of ours, you seemed not to know how to carry it further. Earlier, you'd learned in just hours an entirely new language of stating wants and needs, when you'd asked me not to give up on you, but still you were not practiced at it. The whole problem between you and Dad was the inability of both of you to talk through tough things. Now I saw. You needed an interlocutor, someone to ask the questions, to interpret. You needed . . . me.

"Mom," I ventured, "I can ask you questions?"

You nodded. Finally, after eons of distrust, you trusted me again! I could have wept again, but again, I had work to do.

"So, Mom, in those early years, you seemed so"—I chose the word carefully and I said it gently—"you seemed so angry. What was it about, all the anger?" And here you surprised me.

You said, "I don't really know, Sis."

"Oh Mom, that's so modern."

"What do you mean?"

"Complicated, confusing, inconclusive."

You nodded and rolled your eyes: "It was complicated." Then you reconsidered. It wasn't so complicated, really. And you revealed a clue.

"You and Larry have a nice partnership."

I reassured you. "You had a nice partnership with Dad at the end, the last twenty-five years."

"Yes, we did," you said. "We enjoyed the traveling."

"But," I ventured, "you wished you'd had that partnership earlier."

You nodded. You described the things I had heard many times before, but this time you were presenting them as your final argument, totaling them up. You were a young mother, yanked from your home in Ohio, raising three children, all alone, no help from Dad, you were overtired much of the time, and when you got overtired you had no bounce, and thus you snapped at us and Dad.

I restated your case. "So, there you were, the young mother, raising three *very* lively kids, you were overworked and overtired most of the time—not just much of the time but most of the time—and you sure would have appreciated more help from your husband, your partner. Since your husband and partner wasn't around all that much, that made you your children's taskmaster and you didn't appreciate being made the meanie, while Dad got all the glory."

You nodded emphatically. "That's really it."

I added, "Not fair, is it?"

"Not very," you said, "but I don't want to crab about it."

I then asked you, "Was being a mother enough for you? Larry always comments on your executive abilities." What I wanted to know was, was it being a mother that made you angry?

But you said no, all you ever wanted was to be a mother. I said you were a splendid mother,

"And you took it so seriously." You picked up on the "seriously." You said you knew Dad loved his family, but you sometimes wondered if his medicine was more important to him than us . . . than you.

I said, "I can see how you would think that, Mom. And I can see how it would make you angry." By now I had reached across and taken your hands. I felt us descending from our long-anticipated summit; I felt us relaxing. So I felt safe to venture, one last time, into the No Man's Land that I once occupied between you and Dad. "Mom," I said, "I hope that my getting between you and Dad did not prolong our struggle." God said we must protect the meek, and while I hated calling Dad meek, when it came to you, the possibility of losing you, he was meek, so vulnerable. "He loved you so much, Mom, and he was so afraid of losing you. That must have been why he was always asking me, 'Why is she so hostile?'" If I was "being used," as you said, if I was the means of bringing you two back together, then I would sacrifice myself. I did not like doing it—it made for a frightening childhood, but I would do it for my parents.

You said you could see me "getting roped in" by Dad and you did not like it, "not one little bit." But, again, you felt outnumbered, helpless against the powerhouse team.

"So, Mom," I smiled, "after all is said and done, we were both right. We both had our reasons, our *good* reasons. We were both right."

Brightening at this new thought, you said, "That's right."

You really liked me saying we were both right. Everyone needs their moral purpose understood. You gave me a lovely smile and relaxed. "Isn't this interesting, Mom," I said, "Dad always said, about diagnosing a disease, 'Look for the simplest possible answer.'"

I thought of what Dad said to me in Hawaii, about childhood being a "happy time." I sketched the scene and told you I had responded to him that my childhood was not a happy one.

You said, "I did not know that," but whether you meant you did not know Dad thought that about childhood, or my childhood, or what he had said to me—no matter.

I needed—we needed—to lighten up now. "You know, Mom," I said, "if I'd had a different childhood, I might have been, you know"—I laughed—"normal." We laughed together. I added that I got many good things out of my struggle, "eventually."

Using the laughter, I said, "Bet you thought this scene was going to be one big dramatic shouting match. Shoot-out at the O.K. Corral." You laughed. I added, "Good thing your daughter is so—-"

You chimed in smartly, "Talkative. You're *so* talkative."

"Verbal, Mom, I'm verbal—and it's all your fault."

I have replayed this scene, so many times in my mind's theater, Mom, and laughed and cried and marveled at what we did.

On the way home, Larry said, "That was amazing," and I said, "I know, I know, I know." From then on, from that evening forward, you and I were—at long, long last—our true selves with each other. I had gotten my mother back; you had gotten back your daughter. It took a long, long time, but aren't we glad we lived to see this, truly for us, New Day?

Of course, immediately after this summit of truth telling—when just about all in our joint history had been revealed—I was leveled by a one-two punch of a thought. *If there was such a simple explanation to Mom's harsh behavior toward Dad in those early years, why was my reaction so complicated, so galvanic, so not simple? Had all my suffering in those early years been . . . unnecessary?*

This recognition, that one's suffering may have been unjustly exacted, can be crazy-making to some. It drove Electra to kill her mother Clytemnestra as payback for her mother murdering her father, an act prolonging an endless tragic cycle. But *moi?* I now had to laugh; I *had* to. The gods, I now saw, had had their fun with this mortal being—it's called Life, living a life, dealing with its trials and tribulations. I think the gods were a tad unfair playing havoc with a child. But the child survived, she learned, adapted, and prevailed. And, instead of vanquishing her former nemesis, she made peace with her. *Break the tragic cycle*—with understanding, with love.

Mom, your arc in this drama can be explained simply as an overworked mother, functionally without a partner, snapping at her beloveds in her exhaustion, reacting (as I see now) rather than provoking. My arc is similarly simple: a child who sensed something off between her parents, and though she misread the cause because nobody explained it to her, she tried to fix things by playing referee and shielding her father, the less able combatant, against her mother's anger.

Would that child do it all over again, knowing all the suffering and loneliness to come? I said earlier that, no, I could not. But to save her soul—make that Soul—yes, that child, seeing her father suffering, would *have* to do it all again. It *was* the right thing to do. And yet, what a conundrum. I think of that time in my life, and *I simply do not know how I survived*, without explainer, without protector or comforter, and nobody running interference for me.

This is the part that can still tip me back into anger. I love that brave little girl, that questing young woman, wrestling her conundrum. How could the traumatized child forget the ugly flashpoints: the night Dad tried to drag you from my bed; the night you vowed divorce and I begged Dad not to abandon us. And decades later, your dumping on me as an "unloving daughter who had it so easy." Again, the gods laughed at "so easy."

Our next visit, I asked you about the first of those flashpoints when Dad tried to drag you from my bed. I asked you if you remembered it.

Significantly, you said, "Vaguely."

And equally significantly—and somewhat surprisingly, as

for decades I had expected a confrontation wherein I on behalf of my child-self would demand an apology—I, in that moment, decided *not* to pursue that flashpoint, nor the other two. Because if I had brought all my powers of argumentation to bear in a confrontation with you about those traumatic (to me) flashpoints, if I had "thrust home" as Cyrano de Bergerac might, I could see I would likely "win," and by winning I would reduce you to shame and humiliation, for much was conveyed in your "Vaguely." You knew you were on shaky, maybe indefensible ground. But by so reducing you, I would also strip you of your moral mandate, and what is a mother without her moral mandate? Moreover, I would be pushing my own moral integrity over the line, into moral righteousness. I stepped back from that fight.

The dramatist in me was aware I was leaving rich material unexamined, but the humanist in me overruled the dramatist. Besides, what would such "examination" yield? You had just given me the key, the simple explanation of your behavior in those early years—anger and exhaustion. I could see how anger and exhaustion could account for all three flashpoints. And in an "aha" moment of recognition, I suddenly saw the third flashpoint—when, caring for your ailing husband whom you knew was dying, you, beyond angry and beyond exhausted, called me "an unloving daughter who had it so easy"—you were caught up in terrible, terrible suffering, the kind of crazy-making, lethal suffering of the ancient Greek tragedies. In that moment, you were saying you were "done" with me and in angry reaction I declared I was "done" with you. The Furies *nearly* had their final victory.

But we, Mom, you and I, we closed the door on the Furies— forever—when we stepped back from the brink; when we assured each other that we did not see each other as evil; when we confessed to each other that we were lonely without the other; your astonishing action when you stepped far out of character and made yourself so vulnerable, by asking me not to give up on you; and now me, deciding not to prosecute the long-anticipated trial to establish my innocence and your guilt.

Conflict resolved, conflict resolved, conflict resolved. One by one we vanquished them, Mom, getting to peace.

I am so proud of us, so happy, and not a little amazed.

Over the phone around this time, finding ourselves in purr-fect agreement over some topic—I remember this exchange exactly—I said, "Oh Mom, I think Dad would be pleased for us."

"Yes," you said, "he saw the rage in us"—I don't ever recall your using the word "rage" before—"and he didn't know what to do."

I said, "We had to learn to trust each other again, not see each other as opponents and really trust that both of us wanted harmony."

Once past the swirling maelstrom of rage and anger, people can *finally* look back and see—with the clarity that in no way is possible while they're in the maelstrom—how rage and anger distort the circumstances, derange the combatants, and spin the conflict out of control. Shakespeare said anger makes us deaf; it also makes us blind and heartless.

In my mind's eye (an image coined by Shakespeare), I see two figures in a landscape, two women, looking down at the mael-strom from the safety of a highland, observing all the world's rage and anger swirling on the plain below. They turn to each other, smile, and—with gladdened hearts and both now in possession of a new lens on life—they head off, together at last, toward the light, toward the upper air.

What things have I learned from our struggle? Let me count the ways, briefly:

One. I can feel in my bones when there's something off in a relationship or a situation. Rather than live with that tension, as many people can, I am able to address it. Able? I am completely unable *not* to address it, to try to fix it. If there is a python under the carpet, I feel driven to address it, otherwise pythons do kill.

Two. No matter what hard things there may be in one's life—a primal relationship that's "off," a divorce—those hard things cannot be the excuse for self-destructive behavior and certainly they cannot be allowed to sculpt our character. We must be our own sculptor, our own Rodin, shaper of the most precious of all possessions: our character—a lesson I intuited as a child in that No Man's Land between you and Dad. While some people acknowledge they are the direct product of their parents, I crafted myself *apart*. I had my own sculptor's studio.

Three. Witnessing Dad's suffering and wanting to alleviate it made me of one heart with the world's suffering—from (in my childhood) the Hungarian Revolution when citizens battled Soviet tanks, to the siege of Sarajevo when people were targeted running through Sniper's Alley, to the epic suffering today of huge refugee populations on the move, as well as the suffering of our fellow Americans whose lives have been wrenched in a globalizing job market. This heart does more than pump.

Four. Closely related is my ability and willingness to make the moral point, in commentary and elsewhere in public. This capacity flows from my formative years prosecuting Dad's case against you for abuse of power, which prosecution became for me a moral crusade. Out of moral justice, I still wield the sword-arm on the underdog's behalf. But moral distinctions must be made. The French saying "To understand all is to forgive all" is . . . well . . . wrong. Not everything the human heart wants is permissible, and I am willing to draw the line. This gets me in trouble with my fellow liberals, but life's most important matters are moral, and with my early prosecutorial role against my moral arbiter—you—I engage, as a veteran. From early trauma, *the* most important gift—a moral compass—was salvaged.

Five. Having battled with you, the all-powerful mother whom I once feared with a fear Emily Dickinson described as "Zero at the Bone," and having survived our battle, I am far, far stronger—warrior strong—than had I had a "normal" childhood. There is little I fear in human relations; I fear no one. I feel at one with humanity.

Six. And I am verbal. Trying to figure out what was "off" between you and Dad set me on the path of active questioning, rumination, passionate feeling. If I hadn't acquired the ability to externalize and give voice to everything on my mind and in my heart, I would have been sunk, become as you'd say a "jibbering idiot." Of course being verbal helps with being a writer.

All these capacities I once deployed against you, I now redirect to the world. Where once I approached you, figuratively, with my hands before me, to shield myself, I now come arms at my side or, often, around you. Now in our photos together, my arm around you has a grip to it, like I'd captured something precious (I had). I think of the origin of the handshake: to show neither person has a weapon. Being verbal, I could go on here how our primal relationship affected me—it being primal, how could it not?—but I want to get back to *our* story, Mom, yours and mine.

All our excavating, our reclamation work, you and I did in the first two years of my return, 2002–2003, which gave us a good fifteen years as true mother and daughter. Being a mother first and always, you continued fearlessly to exercise your maternal prerogative—the prerogative authorizing you to tell your children what to do, even when they were adults with graying hair. Now, in our Renaissance, I used humor to push back. "Now, Millie, don't be so bossy," which seldom did the job. You would rephrase and try again. And I would rephrase and push back more, laughing. "Mom, your hand—it's on my tiller. Take it off, please." If further clarification were needed, I'd say, "Clearly, Mom, you missed the class in power-*sharing*."

Larry would laugh and shake his head: "You two . . ."

Relaxing even more, I attempted some self-deprecation. Grandma was the first person I knew who engaged in this endearing trait. Even as a child, I noticed whenever she'd shake her head at some "dumb" thing she'd done and chide herself ("Oh Gwen"), she seemed a bigger person for it. Interesting physics: deflation leading to inflation. Larry also practices this trait. But for this exercise to work, certain rules apply.

You didn't grasp these rules immediately. When I tried out my first instance of self-deprecation, you pounced on my "stupidity." But now I used mock-anger as rejoinder. "Mom! You can't take advantage of me making myself vulnerable and jump on me. No can do." (I find you can say the hardest-to-say things using mock-anger.)

All credit to you, Mom, you did stop jumping on me. And . . . you even started making fun of yourself, not often but now and then. Amazing, once the blinding anger is pushed aside, the good will can get in.

Of course, whenever we'd have these fun dust-ups, Larry would laugh yet again. "You two."

We came to laugh about, or at least treat lightly, those things that once upon a time set us off . . . like your anger. Once while we were playing double sol—you were in your mid-eighties by then, early in our rehab—you spoke of your anger in those early years, and I said, "Well, you can't say volcanic anger has hurt your longevity!" We laughed at that crack, hard and long. I heard lots about how I'm not "normal," but since you and I had achieved normalcy in our relationship, I took no offence. I heard lots about how verbal I was. Once at dinner with you, I noted how, as a teenager, I was so self-conscious that I had to ask my mother to ask the waiter for more water.

You looked over at Larry. "*That's* not her problem now, is it?"

Three-way laughter.

We even went shopping—once—that commercial activity symbolic to many (me included) of what mothers and adult daughters do if they are close. Though you always made your own clothes, you thought you'd treat yourself and buy an outfit for some upcoming event. We met at Tacoma Mall at Nordstrom. You had me come into the fitting room with you because you wanted my advice. You were trying on the slacks to a pantsuit, but, as you were on the short side (5'4"), the pants, too long, pooled around your feet. I started giggling and couldn't stop.

"Mom, they look like elephant feet!" I blush to relate this, but I wet my pants and had to skitter off to the restroom, like a crab in distress.

You were giggling, too, but you didn't have to skitter. Later, like close mothers and daughters do, we adjourned to dine together for an early dinner. You had fun repeating, "I can't take you anywhere, can I."

You soon were called on to act the comforting mother—for a hard reason—when I was diagnosed with cancer in May 2005.

I was not really surprised when I was diagnosed, because I had been under tremendous nervous stress for the year prior. When the news hit in May 2004 that US troops in Iraq were engaging in torture of Arab detainees at the prison named Abu Ghraib, I instantly felt acute shame for our country, which for so long had been an international champion of human rights. Writing from that feeling, within hours I emailed a letter to *The New York Times*, which was published.

"On behalf of all Americans who feel acute shame, as I do, at the reprehensible actions of the benighted few in our armed forces, President Bush should issue an apology to the Arab world. A great nation acknowledges its errors."

Across the Kitchen Table

At the time I was writing commentary for the *Christian Science Monitor*, and the *Monitor* invited me to write on torture as much as I cared to. I cared, intensely. I wrote a piece titled "Abu Ghraib and the Mirror," about how a degraded American culture could spawn such behavior, even laugh about it. With time it became clear that torture at Abu Ghraib and at other "black" sites was not the action of a benighted few, but was official policy, complete with legal justification in abrogation of the Geneva Conventions. I wrote about each ugly revelation, including how our torture policy put our own troops in jeopardy, if they were captured, of being tortured themselves.

I was on fire—with shame and nausea—for America. You saw me in this state. You heard me when I said I felt I was on fire, like my "nervous grid" was electrified. You became alarmed, and after dinner one evening when I had carried on, again, about America's moral fall, you spoke this wise counsel.

"Sissie, we know you feel. But can you feel a little less? You're going to hurt yourself."

I have since taken your counsel and cooled off considerably. Now I visualize my nervous grid as a treasure chest over which my guardian angel must ward off with her sword-arm all stress.

But by then the damage had been done, one year's worth of non-stop electrification. We got the diagnosis—thyroid cancer—in early May. Surgery was scheduled mid-month to remove the thyroid.

But I did not tell you right away. Your eighty-fifth birthday was coming up on the thirteenth, and we had long-laid, eagerly anticipated plans to celebrate it at our house with all the family coming—J.C. and Sue, Ted and Jan, Sue's sister Miki and husband Joe. I did not want to spoil your happiness—who was the one most eagerly anticipating this event but the Birthday Girl?—so I decided to tell you afterward.

At your birthday dinner, you were the happiest I had ever seen you—vivacious, laughing, and relaxed. For eighty-five, you were still so beautiful. The photos of you blowing out your candles on the triple-decker chocolate cake Larry baked, of you with your arms around your children—they are ones for the album. You beamed.

Next day, when I called you, I knew my news would throw you, which was exactly the word you used. "Mom," I started out, "I am really, really sorry to tell you this, but . . . I have cancer." There was a long silence.

Finally, you stammered, "Sissie, I have to get off the phone. I'll call you right back."

When you called back a half-hour later, you said you were thrown and needed to pray and collect yourself. However, you still sounded rattled. You asked if we had gotten a second opinion; we had. You asked why the rush to surgery.

"Because my doctor wants to catch the ENT surgeon she thinks so highly of before he retires. Might as well get on with it." I added I held off with the news so as not to ruin your birthday.

Then, the woman who never complained about the unfairness of life, said, "This isn't fair."

"It sure isn't, Mom." It hung in the air, what we were both thinking: Mother and daughter, after decades apart, recently reconciled—would the happy times be cut short too soon? Going against the natural order, would the one eliminated be the daughter?

What you said next moved me to my depths. You said, "The happiest day of my life, followed by the saddest."

You choked up; I thought you would cry. I could hear it. My mother loved me—to her depths. I became so inspired, I started manufacturing courage on the spot.

"Mom," I declared, "I am going to beat this—just you watch—and we are going to have many more happy years together, you and I. Fear not, dammit! We will fear not!" You did not correct my profanity. Larry and I had studied up on it, thyroid cancer was not the worst cancer, not like ovarian or lung cancer; if you had to get a cancer, this was the one to get. "It is *not* a death sentence."

On the day of surgery, you prayed for me from home. J.C., Ted, and Joe would be with Larry in the waiting room. You asked me to call beforehand. I called enroute to the hospital, from atop our famous Narrows Bridge, spanning the currents of the Puget Sound separating Tacoma and Gig Harbor. It was I who suggested we pray, saying the Twenty-third Psalm. We started out together. "The Lord is my shepherd, I shall not want. He maketh me to lie down in green pastures, he leadeth me beside the still waters. He restoreth my soul." When we got to "Yea, though I walk through the Valley of the Shadow of Death," you had to stop. I carried on, injecting as much steel into my voice as I could. "I will fear no evil, for thou art with me, thy rod and thy staff they comfort me." I wobbled when I said, "My cup runneth over," but I made it home free. "Surely goodness and mercy shall follow me all the days of my life, and I will dwell in the House of the Lord forever." I did not point out it was the pagan, not the churchwoman, who remembered her scripture. But then, the churchwoman was thrown, and the pagan was girding herself for the knife.

Living with cancer for years now—I do wish I were "clean" from it—I maintain this bravado. It can be more than mere show; constant practice becomes an attitude, aiding and abetting the life instinct. Actually, it is the same bravado you yourself exhibited with your uterine cancer. As you said, cancer "just wants to scare us and we can't let it."

When my cancer recurred, in 2010, you were thrown again. "Why did it have to come back?" But as a nurse you knew, if just one cancerous cell remained, it could metastasize into more, which was the case. The surgeon estimated that, during the six-hour surgery, he removed a billion cancerous cells from my neck and lymph nodes. The recovery was excruciating. You called every day, exuding warm mother love.

"You hang in there, Sis." To prevent further metastasis, my Synthroid dosage was upped as high as my body allowed. I fought the fatigue by going to the gym daily.

In the years since, you expressed your admiration. "You are being very brave, Carla." Once, I harked back to my childhood, noting that, projecting ahead from the beset little girl that I was, I might now have given in to the fright and the opera. "But you really have to barrel past that, don't you, Mom, you have to be like steel. Like you." You said you weren't so sure you were all that steely. Besides, you said, "you have to live with this cancer the rest of your life." But maybe not. You were pleased I connected with Seattle's Fred Hutchinson Cancer Center. Fingers crossed that an experimental drug trial there will someday vanquish my cancer. I hold fast to what Dad said: "Carla Nan, do you know what they're going to cure next?" Until the cure, I live life to the fullest.

Still, Mom, I cannot imagine trekking through cancer's Valley of the Shadow of Death if you and I were still alienated, if we were still lost to each other. All bravado aside, I cannot imagine it.

Because we had been alienated for so long, we had to update each other on vast expanses of our lives. Our way of doing that turned out to be storytelling: telling the story of how we got from A to B to C in any given chapter. Woven into the storytelling were our justifications for what we did. The storyteller, hand on her own tiller, told her story *and* defended it, without much in the way of cross-examination. You might say we were explaining ourselves to each other.

Much of this explaining happened over double solitaire.

You filled in more of your biography, the early part. You disclosed your mother did not want you to follow in her footsteps, to be a "farmer's wife"; she wanted you to go out into the world. Interesting that my main memory of Grandma was as a jovial woman, her entire body rocking with laughter. Her wish to see you leave the farm must have been a comment on how difficult it was for her and your father to keep the farm going during the Great Depression, and also the relief she felt to have survived it—thus the joviality, the laughter.

"I think so," you said.

Thus we conjure our notions to explain the mystery of others, the essential mystery at our core and, most especially, of family.

Staying on the topic, I noted, "It must be nice to have your mother's blessing," her approval of whatever you chose to do with your life. "Mom," I said, "I never wanted to be an English teacher," which was always your goal for me; I always wanted to be a writer. "Without your *Good Housekeeping* seal of approval, I had to make my own way."

To which you replied, "You've done okay, haven't you?"

I agreed. I said whatever I had accomplished—the civil rights career, the writing career—I took full credit for it, since I lacked a mother bravoing me on. It couldn't have been pleasant for you to hear, but you did not object; it was fact.

"Just don't whine about it," you said.

"I don't think I do," I said. I hated a whining voice in my head.

Especially the civil rights career, my emergence as a feminist, you never did approve; you continued to think of feminists as troublemakers. But as I explained—more explaining, more close listening—historically speaking, the generations now changed so much, one from another, more than in previous times when the generations carried on the same line of work, customs, and the ethos of their predecessors. "That's true," you said, so I continued. With the generations changing so much, they had their own descriptors—greatest generation, silent generation, boomers, etc. Your generation, the greatest, was indeed the greatest, I believe. As a boomer, I thought our mission was to honor what you had achieved—survived the Great Depression, waged World War II and won—and then build on it. Greatest as your generation was, there were oversights: racism, sexism, anti-Semitism. Given our early struggle, yours and mine, about the rightness and wrongness of things, it was guaranteed that I would go out into the world and try to right the wrongs I found there, starting with civil rights.

"It was a Fate we ourselves made, Mom." I could see my explaining was penetrating. "What seems like defiance against the mother may be the daughter's effort to participate in the events of her time or else feel she missed out."

Your response? "Hmmm."

Besides, Mom, how many times did I hear you say, "It's a man's world"—and you did not say it happily. You thought women "organized things better," were "more down to earth"; you spoke of wanting your voice heard. "When's *my* time?"—the lament I heard from you so often in the early years when once again Dad was a no-show and you were sole parent—was a classic feminist lament. You would take exception to the word "lament," but what else was it? You acknowledged the "dumb" strictures on women, yet we are not supposed to "make trouble?" You were . . . conflicted, to say the least. Face it, Mom, you were a feminist in disguise.

And if we did have to refer to our earlier struggle—your tensions with Dad, my tensions with you—we did so gently. We could say—amazing, now I think back on it—"I was so hurt" when such-and-such occurred, and the other would listen and take it onboard, like it was regular baggage. It was over double sol that you admitted "other people knew" there were "problems" between you and Dad. Over play, I said, "Oh really, who?" and you told me. Sometimes, to avoid reigniting the old battles, I resorted to humor. Invoking Charlie Brown from the *Peanuts* cartoon, I said, "Good grief, Mom, without your counsel and advice,

I had to navigate puberty on my own." Which produced a *Huh* in me. Joking about what once was combustible between the two of us—was trivialization actually a disservice, a blasphemy of all our earlier suffering? Was Shakespeare right? Life is either tragedy or comedy?

Life, I have come to think, is a mix of both tragedy and comedy, plus the unexpected and the uncategorizable. It is a collage.

For the most part, we achieved in our last fifteen years together an easy flow, easy laughter, easy silences. What an achievement! Together we melted the ice that separated us for so long, and we drank of the flowing waters.

How strange! I see now that the question I put to you most forcefully, over and over, demanding an answer—*What was I supposed to do when you attacked Dad? Stand by?*—we actually never addressed per se in our rehab, we never deconstructed it even in the freer, more self-revealing discussions in our last fifteen years together. Certainly, the question for me—to be complicit or not in the commission of a moral injustice—was not rhetorical or empty; it was—still is—central to my view of myself as a moral being. I am a stand-up person, I do not stand by.

Pursuit of an answer must have been set aside and become moot when I decided not to probe further your vague recollection of the past traumas, when I decided to forgive you, when the dramatist in me gave way to the humanist. I realize I am sounding vague here myself, but so thoroughly satisfied was I with our work in rehab that I never made a mental note to, next time, press Mom on the stand by point.

Perhaps only in the innermost chambers of our heart do we ponder the moral character of our beloveds. I never had to doubt your character, Mom. Had I pursued the stand by question with you, no doubt you would have had to say, "No, I did not expect you to stand by and be morally complicit," and I could have crowed, "Then I was right all along!" But while I needed that merit badge of the stand-up moral being to acquit myself in life, I did not want that final victory against you. I wanted us to remain moral peers.

We had many discussions about moral questions, many relating to my commentaries, when I discussed with you the difficulty of making the moral point in what I called our Brass Age, when America had lost its moral compass. You liked those discussions, you had a lot to contribute to them, and though you did not say it, you signaled, *You keep a-goin', Sis.*

Everybody wants a pat on the back from their mother. I feel I got mine, finally.

Joe—whom Larry and I consider our best friend—said to me recently something I have continued to ponder. With his typical wisdom, he said, "The question for Millie was, always, 'Can you carry the water?' Can you acquit yourself in life, not only in the day-to-day but in the moral?" Closing the loop, Joe said he knew you—Millie—knew that I—Carla—could indeed carry the water and, ultimately, you were well-pleased with your daughter.

I thought, *Even though, long ago, I had to carry the water against my own mother.* Happily we ended up carrying the water together.

Life . . . it's *so* complicated, but so compelling. Who knew this would be our story?

Two issues you returned to with some frequency were children and the Church. Sometimes we talked about them while playing double sol, sometimes we would have to stop play.

Children. You still wished Larry and I had had children. "Any child would have been fortunate to have you two as parents," you said. You worried we would be alone in our old age, not looked after, as your children were looking after you. I suppose it was helpful for you to express your regret about not getting your deepest desire—grandchildren—but it hurt me to go there. In explaining again, I cast our decision as one of logistics driven by the US Navy. Larry was gone far more than Dad; I would have been the fulltime mother, angry. If you prodded further, I cited your example. "With Dad not around to help out, you were not always a happy mother." You'd demur, "I was happy," and I had to say, gently, "No, Mom, you were not. I was there. I saw." You'd add, also gently—you and I were being *so* careful—"You exaggerated," and I'd shift to clinical language to prevent us from sliding back into the "bad old days."

"If I did exaggerate, it was because my mother was not *available* to me to explain things." I was never sure you understood. But to ensure complete understanding, I simply could not replay the whole awful opera and lay the onus for it—my unhappy childhood, my understandable (at least to me) disinclination to repeat it with children of my own—at your feet. Again, it was home-grown fate, born of our tangled past. The closest I came to revealing the truth was to say, "*If* we could have gotten our train back on the track, you and I . . ." On the baby question, I never got to the table; I never truly even got into the room.

If you continued sighing, which was understandable, I felt sad for my mother's heartache. I stopped with the cards and said: "Mom, I can assure you, it was *not* a happy decision. Larry and I did not skip around saying, 'Whee, we are child-free!'" I also said, several times, that I was sorry my branch of the family tree ended with me. In the cycle of Life, it was a grave thing to say no.

Trying to boost you up and reduce your heartache, I would quote you back to yourself. I reminded you that you often said, "Children change a marriage"; I did not want my excellent marriage changed. You also said, "Get happy with what you've got." I am, truly, happy. And, once and only once, I said, "Mom, now that I can confide in you—something I am so grateful for—have

I confided to you that our decision not to have children was a mistake?"

You paused and shook your head.

"So, Mom," I said, taking your hands in mine, "we need to get happy about this, lay this decision to rest."

I have two godchildren, who both as adults asked me to be their godmother. It is enough.

Church. You "grieved" (your term) about my drift from the Church. The reasons for my drift from religion—organized religion, that is, not religion itself, nor God—are many (its politicization, for one), are shared by millions, and could take a book. Basically, they have to do with a moral institution failing its pilgrims. I wanted a fighting church that took a stronger stand against war (Vietnam, Iraq), against torture (Iraq again), and did better by women, fighting for our full equality. You thought the pilgrims themselves were more at fault, becoming less moral, and I will grant you that. The moral fiber of American society has degraded.

Another reason for my drift: This point was the hardest to discuss, because it would be the most hurtful to you, but we did, reaching peace. I described how, from my viewpoint as that young and frightened child, it *appeared* that the practitioner of Christianity nearest to me—that is, you—personified religion's most regular failing: hypocrisy—saying the right thing while doing wrong. (See: your treatment of Dad.) I said "appeared" because, in the arena where our early drama took place, it seemed the case. You the churchwoman, violating, in your attacks on Dad, the Church tenets of kindness and charity. This casting of you as a hypocrite was, as I stated—you had to look down to compose yourself—"the most grievous damage done to you, Mom, and I am sorry that that happened. Will you forgive the child who got it wrong?"

You nodded, not able to speak.

I went on. Now that I knew you were not a hypocrite, but

rather an overworked and exhausted mother who just wanted more help from her husband and partner, I said, "I am so, so glad to retire that misperception of you, Mom. I am so glad to see you"—now I had trouble speaking—"as the good, good person you are." I added, "Same for me, please."

Recalling this exchange—is it okay, Mom, to be amazed at us? At this point, our game of double sol had long since stopped.

Having now established you were not a hypocrite, still, my early antipathy toward such types, whether in the Church or out in society, has stayed powerfully with me and has prejudiced me against organized religion. But, as I promised you, I will stay "open" to the possibility of returning to the fold—as Dad did late in life. I can see how, as one grows older, the Church can comfort.

I regret now that, in my forty years apart from you, I did characterize you to the world as that worst thing, a hypocrite, mainly during my early adulthood when I was flailing. It was then I learned how many people have problems with their parents—their mother usually—and how much the world is at odds with its own.

It is my great pleasure now to inform the world—the forthcoming is a joke, Mom—of your miraculous and total conversion. But as I stressed with you any number of times, while I may have reservations about the Church, I never had any doubt about the need to develop and live a moral life. This pilgrim has endeavored to follow the Biblical precepts—the Golden Rule, the Ten Commandments, the Sermon on the Mount, etc.

It was in our early struggle, a struggle I saw being about right and wrong action, that I came to this commitment to a moral life: I knew we were playing in deadly earnest, what Italians call *sul serio*, and I knew I needed to take the right action or do damage to my conscience.

Living a moral life, living conscientiously, and writing about it in increasingly amoral times has been highly challenging, but then, this pilgrim has grown robust. Moreover, it is a joy to live with a man who is similarly robust morally.

So, just as you nearly wept when I said I no longer saw you as a hypocrite, you came to see us no longer as pagans. Not that you ever called us pagans, but the impression was there. One needs one's moral purpose understood. I could tell from the way you looked at us, we were understood.

Finally, there was another theme that recurred between us—politics—and it recurred because we were on opposite sides. You were on the right, I am on the left, more specifically, center-left. You felt outnumbered, because Larry is center-left, too. Like many families, we took and defended our positions without much in the way of explaining the evolution of our thinking or how we got there in the first place.

In increasingly polarized times such as ours, with the right and the left coming to view each other as aliens, even un-American or the enemy, more energy goes into holding one's position and even less into explaining. I am glad that, in our Renaissance, we broke the impasse, you and I, and finally got to explaining our politics to each other. We did not convert each other, but we did turn down the heat. It was you who forced the issue.

It was during the Iraq war, two or three years into it, with President George W. Bush presiding. We were at your house for another Thanksgiving dinner; the family gathered around your dining room table. I referred earlier to my being verbal, but your whole family is verbal—and opinions on the war and Mr. Bush were expressed pointedly and passionately. In my own passion, I did not notice you had gone silent. Later, as everybody was leaving, you asked me—ordered me, actually—to stay behind. We slipped into our usual places at the kitchen table and you unleashed.

You were not happy, "not one little bit," that your Thanks-giving dinner, which you had worked so hard over, had been dominated by nothing but "Bush-bashing," and clearly I was the ringleader.

"Just a minute, Mom, we all hate this war"—an unnecessary war, waged on the false premise of weapons of mass destruc-tion, with torture served on the side—"and we bash Bush because he not only got us into it, but he is keeping us there for who-knows-how-long."

Always the mother, your real upset was on behalf of Bush's mother Barbara: How would she feel knowing her son was being bashed at Thanksgiving tables across the land that day?

"Mom," I said, gently, "how do you think the mothers of our troops who were killed there feel today?" I appealed to your his-toric stance, the one I heard all my life: "I hate all war."

Unmollified, you recurred to your charge that I was the ring-leader in a more general sense. I "poisoned" my brothers' minds and turned them both Democratic.

"Dad and I raised you kids to be Republican. What happened?"

As it was getting late, I did not engage your question fully but resorted to platitude, noting the right that every American held dear: Think for themselves. I also noted, while J.C. was fiercely Democratic, Ted split his vote, "so your side gets one-half a body"—a response more partisan and glib than helpful. On our way out, I said, "At least you can say your children are not apathetic."

But I thought about your question, "What happened?" Sev-eral nights later I called you with my thoughts.

"Think about it, Mom," I said. "When we—J.C., Ted, and I—were coming along, coming into the age of awareness, John F. Kennedy was President. You didn't like Kennedy—you dis-trusted the Kennedy glamour—but Kennedy made public service exciting, even noble." I cited my childhood friend Jack, who heard the call and went into the Peace Corps. Then came Lyndon Johnson. In addition to enacting Medicare and Medicaid, Johnson got America to do what it long needed to do—pass the Civil Rights Act of 1964 and the Voting Rights Act of 1965. Your daughter, as soon as she got out of college, went into civil rights work, making good on a vow she made years earlier. "Mom, remember Proffitt's department store in Centralia? You and I were there shopping for my high school graduation, and on the TV—there was a wall of TVs—there was Bull Connor, in Birmingham, siccing police dogs and aiming fire hoses against Black people, children included—the children were petrified. In that moment, Mom, I knew what I was seeing was evil and I vowed, 'If ever I get the chance, I will help right that wrong.'" I paused. "And you thought we were just shopping. Your daughter heard the call."

The other end of the line was quiet. "Mom, you there? I can't hear you breathing."

"I'm here," you said. "I'm listening hard."

I went on. "True, Johnson was undone by the Vietnam War, but we all, the whole family, were against that war. Then came Richard Nixon, who extended the war and lied about it, just as he lied about Watergate—-"

Here, I could hear you bristle: Nixon was a favorite punching bag of your daughter's.

"Mom, this is not a defiance thing. I know you were chair of the county Committee to Re-elect Nixon and I know you cherish your thank-you note from the Nixons. But think about it. After Watergate—the criminal act but, even more, the cover-up—that was when the American people began to lose trust in government. Isn't that right?"

You actually agreed! "Well, that's true," you said.

I rested my case: The history your children lived through shaped their political preferences. You accepted that explanation, and political discussion between us became much easier. Still partisan, but less inflamed.

You were an old-line Republican conservative, in favor of small government, fiscal responsibility, and vehemently against the welfare state—all positions explained, in turn, by your own history of surviving the Great Depression. I never understood why you didn't embrace Franklin Roosevelt for his social safety-net programs. Your feeling was your folks and you made it through without a helping hand, and it's best if others did the same. Again, you never really got over the Great Depression.

But we were able to find that mythical common ground, politically. Despite your calling me out for the Bush-bashing, you were against the Iraq War. And you agreed with me that America engaging in torture was a grave moral error.

Which touches on more common ground we recognized: We both thought America was losing its moral compass, increasingly unable to distinguish right and wrong, indulging in the crass and sleazy, play-acting with the pathological and criminal. You understood when I described myself as a liberal who protested liberal licentiousness. You heard me out as I railed against cultural lows, like the hit TV series *The Sopranos*, about a mob boss who "whacked" his rivals and took his contrived troubles to a psychiatrist; and another hit series *Breaking Bad*, about a high school chemistry teacher who, learning he had cancer, turns to manufacturing meth to provide for his family "after." How often I heard you cry out after yet another sex scandal or act of gun violence, "What is happening to us?"

We both echoed Hamlet—"O what a falling-off was there."

This was when I felt closest to you, Mom. Our struggle in its essence had been over the moral compass, *Whose interpretation was right?* But once we resolved the problem and forgave each other, we could share the compass. Sharing it, and sharing the same wavelength, we could then look out at the world, atilt on its axis, and solve its problems in wide-ranging discussions together.

It's those discussions I miss the most now. After glaring at each other so long, Mom—harmony, moral harmony.

Not everything was a seminar between us, though this account may make it seem so. Interspersed with the rehab, and increasingly as the years went on, we did things together, enjoyed family gatherings, traveled—we had fun. Because the tension between us was gone, the fun was all the freer.

Your favorite destination, and for Larry and me, was Mount Rainier—"so majestic," as you said. One spring, the first week the park opened, we hatched the idea of a picnic. It was too early, too cold, and you just about froze your "patootie." We thawed out at Paradise Lodge and laughed. On another outing to Rainier, Larry brought along CDs of Welsh men's choirs, which prompted running commentary about your childhood church in Ohio, where—news to me—Welsh was spoken until you were in your teens. You sat in the passenger seat conducting the choir, singing along, happy. Enroute home, you'd always treat us to blackberry pie à la mode at Copper Creek Restaurant. We introduced you to the north side of the mountain, called Sunrise, and picnicked there.

Of course, every trip to Rainier required your story about your mother . . . how, on her first visit, you drove her up to see the mountain. Climbing up the sharp switchbacks, at a stretch where there was no guardrail, you told Grandma, "Look down the drop-off, Mom." And Grandma, a denizen of Ohio the Flat, stiff with fear in the passenger seat, shot back, "Shut up and drive, Mildred."

You took us on an Alaskan cruise—Larry, me, J.C., and Sue. Since Ted and Jan could not make it, you took them later on a cruise to Cabo San Lucas.

And, of course, there were the many drives to see the fall colors.

After so many years away and missing family gatherings, Larry and I have hosted a host of them—and you sparkled at those.

It is now our tradition that we host the family Christmas, for which Larry and I knock ourselves out.

You came in sporting your Christmas sweater, you went away with "so much loot." We did Thanksgivings at your house, until "it got to be too much" for you, then shifted to J.C. and Sue's. Your birthday, in May, was a great reason to gather family midyear, and since Joe's birthday was two days after yours, we did double-birthday celebrations. A special birthday luncheon we hosted included a half-dozen of your women friends from Chehalis, most now gone. Micheline, a French war bride, told of village life under Nazi occupation, a story you'd never heard before.

J.C.'s birthday in June was another reason to gather midyear. We would meet in Portland at a restaurant, after the lunch rush, and sit the afternoon away, talking and laughing.

One time a woman stopped by our table and said, "I know who the mother and daughter are here." She said to me, "You look so like your mother," to which I said, "Lucky me."

You especially loved the family gatherings that went long, with everyone sitting around the table talking. Your stamina was remarkable. Even as you weakened, you could sit for four, five, or six hours at table, while I'd have to get up midway and stretch. Your head was on a swivel, listening to everybody reporting their news, their views. Your comments in our guestbook expressed your joy.

"I love my family more each year" and "This has been the most wonderful day. I am overwhelmed."

Often, while still at table and during a lull, you and I would look at each other and give a special smile of contentment, a smile that said, "We got here . . . nice, isn't it?"

Meanwhile, out in the world, apart from our warm personal realm, there was work to do—oh Lord, was there work to do!

Since 9/11, America the Beautiful, once the world's sole super-power, had been—and still is—flailing wildly, fearfully, angrily, in a kind of fever, a fever propelling extreme reactionary swings of the domestic political pendulum, from the right to the left and to the right again. The sober and philosophical atmosphere prevailing in the immediate aftermath of 9/11 soon dissipated, way too soon, giving way once again to an anything-goes, celebrity culture. Reinventing "normalcy"? Not happening. Rational, thoughtful voices were—and still are—needed.

Endeavoring to be one of those voices, I continued contributing commentary to *The Christian Science Monitor.* Over time, my editors and I scoped out my beat, an expansive one—politics, culture, and ethical-moral issues; my style they called "big-think in a personal voice." Their editorial guidance—that however dark a picture I needed to paint of our increasingly chaotic post-9/11 world, end, please, on a constructive note if not an action plan—accorded with my personal code: Deal with reality, get to a better day.

For the *Monitor,* to try to restore us to sobriety, I wrote, "America, We Need to Talk—*Seriously.*" With America still dazed two years after 9/11, I wrote "Behemoth in a Bathrobe," a column in dialogue. To protect our precious right to free speech, I urged responsible speech. To allay the growing polarization, I urged the French mode of debate (learned from my French room-mate), to attack the idea, not the person; this column sparked a series. I coined the term "conscientious public" and wrote to that public, which, given the tides of war, torture, and malaise, needed bolstering. When Barack Obama was elected, our first African American president, it seemed a New Day. He outlawed torture his second day in office.

After seven years at the *Monitor*, I moved, same beat, to *The Huffington Post*, where I could publish more often. My first column, a year after the 2008 financial crash, was titled "Recovery Without a Reckoning." I wrote often on behalf of Main Street vis-a-vis Wall Street. I reread Herman Melville's *Moby-Dick* and imagined mad Captain Ahab's theory of risk management. Ten years after 9/11, America still flailed. In response, I wrote columns titled "Exceptional Nations Don't Need to Bluster," "Distinguishing Between Can and Should: What a Superpower Should Be Able to Do," and—it needed to be asked—"Is This a Culture That Wants to Save Itself?" Instead of braggadocio, I urged self-criticism; I continued urging responsible speech. The rising suicide rate among veterans of the Iraq and Afghanistan wars inspired my column, "A War's Premise Must Justify the Troops' Suffering." I urged Mr. Obama to rethink using military drones. On the culture side, I urged critics, who are culture's gatekeepers, to mind the gate more conscientiously, work their moral compass more, mind the perilous tilt of the ship of state.

The run-up to the 2016 presidential election, with candidate Donald Trump ditching democratic norms and making openly racist and xenophobic appeals, signaled a dire turn. I called it "the anger election"; I warned against the disrupter with no follow-up plan. Harking back to your generation, Mom, I wrote a column titled "Whatever Happened to the Famous American Ability to Say 'Nuts!' to Charlatans, Crazies, and Fear-Mongers?" When Trump won, I wrote, "A *Breaking Bad* Culture Got Its President."

You tracked your daughter's commentary, the columns stacking up by your recliner in the living room. I featured you twice in print. You were tickled with "My Republican Mother Gives Thumbs-Up to Occupy Wall Street."

"Greed is killing this country," I quoted you saying.

In the other column, written in the aftermath of the horrific massacre of schoolchildren in Newtown, Connecticut, I quoted you grieving, "Those poor little ones, they didn't have a chance." My column was titled "My Republican Mother Says Yes to Gun Control."

About Mr. Trump and what he portended for the Republican party, you alternated between alarm and, the refrain I'd heard from you for some years, just not wanting to think about it anymore.

Out in the world, though, as America continued to flail, Larry and I became increasingly aware that we needed to become more politically active. It wasn't enough to stay well-informed or, in my case, write on politics. So, in 2004 I went to a Democratic precinct caucus, to check out how the apparatus worked—and got myself elected a state delegate for John Kerry for president. That process, and my reports of the excitement of grassroots politics, got Larry intrigued, and he, too, got involved at the local level.

Of course, when the local Democrats learned of Larry's resumé—battleship captain!—they instantly spawned dreams of running him for office, something major, like state representative in the legislature. They were clever about it. Knowing it was the wife who first got into precinct politics and was writing on the subject, the delegation of Dems who came to the house put the question to both of us: "Would one of you run for state rep?"

That was a Saturday morning; they wanted an answer by Sunday evening. Sunday afternoon we went to a movie, and as the lights came down, I leaned over to Larry and said, "Dear, the nation is in trouble, our democracy is in trouble, we *need* to do this—and you're it." When the lights came up two hours later, Larry was in campaign mode, organizing.

And: He won! When I called with the news, "Son of a gun," you said, "now I probably have to call him Honorable."

Thus began Larry's legislative career in the House of Representatives. Whereas before, in the Navy, he was the commanding officer up on the bridge, now he was out among the people—and he loved it. Larry likes people. When he was out, sunup to sundown, meeting with constituents, I called it "tending his parish." When he was offered appointment to the Senate when our senator ran for Congress, Larry declined; he preferred "the people's house." In session, when transacting the people's business, Larry, savvy politician that he became, sought a Republican cosponsor for his bills and almost always won passage. In caucus, he urged his fellow Dems to think strategically and long-term, not easy to do in the heat of political battle. In his third and fourth terms, he chaired the House committee on higher education. His proudest achievement: restarting, post-2008 crash, the state's investment in higher ed.

He loved it all—all eight years. We did not love the way it ended: swept out by the Republican wave in 2014, which carried off every other Democrat in our district. Larry was thrown for a few weeks, saying, "I sure loved being a legislator"—you can do more good for more people as a lawmaker. He loved it all: the legislating, the representing, the campaigning—knocking on doors and asking people their issues—even the fundraising and asking for money.

About the latter, he did run into a wee snag—you, his mother-in-law. "On principle," you felt, as a life-long Republican, you could not "in good faith" make a campaign contribution to a Democrat. Larry laughed about it and used this nugget on the campaign trail. He'd leave you donation envelopes, "to give you the opportunity to change your mind." Finally, you did. In what became Larry's last campaign, you made a donation—for twenty-five bucks! (Confession: I used this particular nugget in my eulogy to you, Mom—and it brought down the house.) Even though not of your party, you tracked carefully what Larry did in the "Ledge."

"Saw you on the TV," you'd say, or "Saw you in the paper."

Often, after a day in session, Larry would turn south, "to go see Mom," rather than turn north to come home. You were surprised, you told us, how upset you were when he lost.

Finally, you accepted it. "I guess everything comes to an end."

Everything does come to an end, eventually—most notably, life.

Of our seventeen-year coming-together, you were energetic and in good health for the first ten years or so. Then, in my nightly phone calls, I began hearing about the "minus-minus-minus"—your strength ebbing away. But as long as you could, you were still the dynamo, or tried to be.

You kept your beauty shop going until six years from the end—you were a working woman into your 90s. Impressive, Mom. Toward the end, with fewer clients, the "lifers," you would adjourn with them to the kitchen for coffee, cookies, and more talk. Even after you hung up your scissors permanently, those same lifers would ring you up in an emergency, so you could "do them up" for a grandchild's graduation or wedding. I loved your cuts, but I eased off early on, as I could see that preparing dinner for us, then a game of double sol, then giving me a trim was becoming too much. You took mild offense when I started getting my cuts elsewhere.

"They don't do your sides right." But I explained I didn't want to overtire you. You appreciated the concern, but you never did approve my 'dos.

On your days off from the shop, you would get antsy and "want to get out and go." You would call up your friend Kay—"Let's go for a drive"—and you'd drive down to the beach or around the county, ending up with dinner at Applebee's or Denny's. Or you'd take day trips, history-oriented, organized by the senior center. Or you'd call up your friends Vi or Virginia to go with you out to the casino. So that you would not blow your children's inheritance at the slot machines, you allowed yourself to play with no more than $100, cash, tucked in an envelope. In time, you went to the casino several times a week for their buffet, to have your hot meal of the day, as you grew weary of cooking for yourself.

Or, occasionally, you would cross out a week or two on your books and take a trip. You loved baseball, specifically the home team, the Seattle Mariners, and several times you flew to Arizona to "check them out" at their spring training. You took two Mississippi riverboat cruises with your friend Shirley, experiences you enjoyed tremendously. Unfortunately, on the second trip you contracted some sort of a bug, resulting in severe pain throughout your whole body. While you made it a point of pride throughout your life never to complain of aches and pains, this time you did. I asked if you had seen your doctor; you had, several days before. Worried about my heretofore uncomplaining mother—had she made it through the night?—instead of my usual evening call, I called in the morning, to ask how you were.

"Oh Sissie," you said, "I hurt so much I can't even pray."

"That's it," I said, "I'm taking you to your doctor." When we saw him—why am I not surprised?—he was surprised to hear of your pain, because you had not told him of it. I shot you a look; you looked away. He diagnosed polymyalgia and prescribed a steroid. I came down again the next day and, lo, a miracle had happened. Within just one day on the steroid, you were pain-free and so happy you raised your walker in the air and were chattier than ever.

"How about a game of double sol?"

But before we pressed on, I had to press home a point. "Mom," I said in my sternest voice, "while we all admire your stalwart spirit, you take this stalwart thing too far." I made you promise that, henceforth, you would let us, your family, know exactly how you were doing and, if not well, how not well. "I am serious, Mom. I want to know how it's going with you. I do not want to be the absent daughter or not in the know. I want to be here for you, Mom, no matter what comes . . ."

You heard the vow I was making, and you agreed. "I will," you said, and you kept your promise. "Now, let's play."

From then on, I heard the "minus-minus-minus" reports, your honest assessment—thank you very much—of how you were doing. You didn't hide your physical frailties behind a stalwart front anymore. Mainly, "minus-minus-minus" meant losing your strength and resilience, your "pep."

"It's getting serious, Sis," you said.

Your son, Ted the nurse, really showed his character now. He checked in on you constantly and, because of his training, knew what he was seeing. He took you to the lion's share of your doctor's appointments; he monitored your meds. He kept J.C. and me informed about your progress, or more accurately, your decline. When he thought you needed in-home care, he did the hiring, only to have you fire whomever was sent.

You were adamant. "I don't want anybody in my home, period." This is about the only time I ever saw my brother show some pique.

Despite the weakening, you continued to make day trips with us—to Mount Rainier, to the Columbia River Gorge for Thanksgiving at J.C. and Sue's house, to Portland for J.C.'s birthday—as long as you could. In your latter years you would beg off, saying you didn't think you could make it, but we always gave you the option. "We'll drop by and if you're able . . ." we'd say. Most of the time, you were ready, you didn't want to miss out.

Franz Kafka, in his final illness at a tuberculosis sanatorium, wrote of his world being reduced, little by little, finally down to "His Majesty the body."

Your world was reducing little by little. With your shop closed, you dropped out of your two bridge clubs, because you did not have the strength to host anymore. I tried to convince you to continue, but you insisted you were done.

More concerning, and a sadder loss for you, you could not make it to church on Sundays. You lacked the strength to park your car in the lot across and down the street, then make the walk to church, especially in rainy weather. I could imagine the loss. Gone was not only the soundtrack of your life—you loved the old hymns—but also the content of your life, the Scriptures, and of course the people there, your church family. You never used the word "adore," but you adored your church family. You made do by reading your Bible at home.

You leaned more on your widow friends—Helen, Kay, Shirley, Vi, Virginia—with whom you said it was so easy to talk "because we're all in the same boat." When any of those friends died, you grieved so. I accompanied you to Virginia's memorial service, but so stricken were you by Helen's death, you could not make yourself go to her service, so I went in your stead. Emily Dickinson said, "My friends are my estate." That expresses it for the value you placed on your friends, and they on you.

Figuratively, one might get out and about with books, by reading. But you did not read much; you were never a reader. Yes, you read my "stuff" but not much else. You watched television instead, a bit too much in my opinion, which I kept to myself. You watched sports. You were killingly funny on "the dumb sports men think up—and they're so serious about them, too." During baseball season, we'd inquire about your Seattle Mariners and ask how "Ichiro" (Ichiro Suzuki) or "Edgar" (Edgar Martinez) were doing; you would give your expert opinion. You'd like knowing that Ichiro was still playing at forty-five and Edgar finally made it into the Baseball Hall of Fame.

Now when we visited, we offered to take you out to dinner or bring dinner with us, to spare you the work. But you usually insisted on cooking. Notwithstanding your general weakening, you still played a fierce game of double sol. The determination to win never left you.

Once over double sol, I paused and said, "Mom, you know that 'main event' between us? I am so, so glad we worked it out." I started to tear up.

You asked, "You're not going to cry, are you?"

"Mom," I said, "I know you still don't believe it, but sometimes tears are called for."

Another visit, I brought a notecard in which I had written you a message of thanks for keeping the family home so long and faithfully as the family steward. You kept that card propped up on your kitchen table for months.

Driving away, we now would turn on the dome light in our car, so you could see both of us waving, blowing you kisses. You stood at the window over the stove, waving back. Once upon a time, you would have turned away quickly to get on with other things. But now you remained at the window, waving—and looking quite alone.

"She's being brave," I'd say to Larry. "Someday she won't be there at the window."

Part Four

The End

In the end, as I said in my eulogy to you, "Mom was right again." You always feared a fall. As a former nurse, you knew that taking a fall was often "the beginning of the end," and in your case, you were right. It happened on a pretty summer day, Tuesday, August 16, 2016.

You were out in your front yard, trying to pull a weed out of the flowerbed under your kitchen window. The weed was a tough one and would not give—until it did—and you fell backward, breaking your left hip. Luckily, a handyman working at the school across the street saw you fall, ran over to you, told you not to move—you wanted to get up (sounds like you)—and he called 911 on his cellphone.

When the ambulance came for you, did you know, I wonder, that you were looking at your beloved home for the last time?

When Ted called me with the news of your fall, I knew immediately it must be something serious, because the call came in the afternoon and family knows not to call me during the workday. I said I wondered if prophecies—your well-known prophesy about taking a fall—were coming true. Ted said he wondered, too.

All three of your children came to see you in the hospital that night. You seemed a bit abashed. *How dare a dumb weed give me a problem?* But you also seemed a bit shut down—the usual can-do spirit was not evident, as if you knew you had begun your final journey.

You sailed through surgery, breathing on your own. At the surgical rehab facility, initially you were diligent about doing the physical therapy, several hours a day, that would get you back to full strength. But after a few weeks, you apparently decided, or perhaps your tired body decided for you, that you were giving up on PT.

I recall coming in one Sunday, early on, and you greeting me with, "I want you to have my rings, Sissie." In your words I heard you making final arrangements, but we weren't there yet. "Momma"—I was now calling you by the name I called you as a child—"I want you to work at PT. We all want you to get stronger. We can talk about rings and stuff later." You spoke of being so tired . . . so terribly tired.

Another time when I arrived, even before I had set down my purse, you told me, in the most authoritative voice you could still command, "I want to go home. Take me home."

"Momma," I said, and tried to sell you on all the assets of the rehab facility: three meals a day, medical care 24/7, "and, very important, PT." You were not having any of it. I knew what you were going to say next.

"You promised."

That was reference to the promise you made me give several times that I would see to it you died in your own home. "Well, Momma, there's a problem," and I explained now you needed a lot of care, 24/7 care. "But all those home-care aides Ted hired for you and you fired? Well"—how could I put this as gently but definitively as possible?—"let's just say, our family is not in good stead with the agency anymore. They wouldn't send us more people even if we begged."

You sank at the news. "Oh."

After that, you stopped speaking of going home, but you didn't really "get happy"—your old directive to us—with what you had: the rehab facility. You got quieter, generally, and became aloof at dinner, so, to assure the nice ladies at table that our family was not stuck-up, I became what you used to call "Chatty Cathy." (It was in chatting up one of your tablemates, Pat, that I learned she'd been kissed by Errol Flynn "back in the day." She said it made her year.)

Of course, in the fall of 2016, the presidential campaign—a campaign like no other in our history, pitting a woman, former Secretary of State Hillary Clinton, against the crude and amoral real estate mogul, Donald Trump—was the main topic at table.

I had strong feelings about Trump and had upped my publication rate expounding on them. I found him a fraud, a racist, and a misogynist, a dangerous proto-autocrat—in sum, a desecration and all-round appalling figure. But I did not share that at your table. Older people in small towns liked Donald Trump.

Finally, after a month of accompanying you to dinner, one of your tablemates, Sharon, asked me, "Carla, what do you think of Donald Trump?"

I ducked and asked, "Oh, I don't know, Sharon. What do *you* think of Donald Trump?"

And Sharon, in her high-pitched voice, declared, "I think he's *terrible*, just *terrible! How* did we get such a terrible choice?"

Whew! "I'm with you, Sharon," I said. Then, seeing the other ladies nodding (nice surprise), I put it to the table as a whole. "How *did* we get such a choice?" adding I thought Trump came as much from our anything-goes culture as from our politics. The ladies agreed.

One lady, Mary, said, "I want to see a woman president before I die."

I was not sure how much you were taking in of these dinnertime conversations, which remained intensely political until the election, and became even more so afterward with Trump's stunning victory. You were past debating and discussion now—you were becoming more quiet at dinner, even occasionally falling asleep.

So, who knew it would be you who brought us some joy, some little relief to our general depression at the ascension of "President" Donald Trump? Who knew it would be—of *all* people—you? I can hear you say, "What'd I do?"

You voted for a Democrat! You voted for Hillary!

Astonishing! Life-long conservative, always but always voted straight-ticket Republican, never voted for a Democrat—in her last election, she voted for a Democrat, a final fact that is even more astonishing than the fact she also voted for a woman. When Ted told me, I thought I wasn't hearing right. He took your ballot to you, read you the candidates, and you announced your decision. "Hillary." When I saw you next, I gave you a huge hug.

"What's that for?" you asked.

I beamed at you and took your hands in mine. "On behalf of American democracy, Mom, thank you!"

Your decision to stop physical therapy was final, despite the pleading of your children. The only time I ever saw Sue cry was over that decision and your reduced quality of life. It was policy at the rehab facility that when a resident stopped showing progress and began to regress, the resident must leave. You had enough residual strength to make it through Thanksgiving and Christmas, but then it was time to move to an assisted-living facility. Ted, as always, was key to that choice, as he knew the area's resources so well. We consulted Dad's old partner, Wayne, who agreed with our choice, Chehalis West.

Just as Dad as a doctor must have known what it meant for his body when he stopped eating, you as a nurse must have known what it meant for your body to stop movement. Very soon after the move to assisted-living, you became wheelchair-bound and bedridden. As if you finally understood the enormity of your decision, you said you would give physical therapy one more try, but by then you could not perform even the most elementary movement, and your request was denied.

"Denial of request" was crushing to all of us. It meant we were now past the Point of No Return, with no hope of getting you back to shore. You had another year of life ahead of you, thanks to your basic sound health, but we knew, and you must have known, too, that—it is crushing to write these words—you were headed out to sea.

Fortunately, your three kids and their spouses were all realists. There was no excuse-making, no "I can't deal with this"; we all dealt. We all revised our lives to be with you. I drove down twice a week, Wednesdays and Sundays; J.C. and Sue, with twice the distance to drive as I had, likewise came up twice a week. And Ted was there most every day; Jan came often, too. So did Larry. You could take pride that one of your children, or one of their excellent spouses, was with you every single day of your final trek. (Meanwhile, Sue and I vowed to each other: If in our old age we fall and break something, we will do our PT.)

Ted moved in furniture from your home—the kitchen table and two chairs; the corner china cabinet complete with some china; your recliner; a dresser on which he set a forest of family photos. Even though it was after Christmas, he decorated your room with Christmas lights. He even brought in the yellow cookie jar, the one whose porcelain lid you could hear from the other side of the house being lifted by one of your brood back in the day.

For myself, seeing you set sail, I did not panic or fall into the Slough of Despond. My overwhelming feeling was one of pride and relief. Our work had been done; we had transacted the "main event" between us. Good thing we had done our work, because this trek we were on now did not allow for much in the way of interaction. Now was the time to show the love—the love that, for so long, had been frozen.

But I was anxious about you. You now bore a worried look all the time, a look you never wore in life. Along with the immobility, your memory suffered. Once, in reference to yourself, you said, "Not bad for eight-five," and I said, "Momma, you are ninety-seven," and you said, "I am?" and made a face. When you chose to talk, you had trouble forming words, which convinced Ted you were having little strokes. And, so unlike you, you were not reading your Bible anymore.

Once I asked you, "Do you talk to God?" and you said, "No." I brought you a copy of the Twenty-third Psalm—"Yea, though I walk through the Valley of the Shadow of Death"—but I did not see you read it.

In your way, Mom, perhaps you were teaching us one last lesson: At the end of life, we pilgrims are terribly alone. And we are terribly fearful. Is that the truth I saw reflected in your worried look? It haunted me then, and it haunts me now, that this is the sorrowful truth you were discovering, and suffering, and could not relay back to us.

Of course, the "minus-minus-minus" of your physical diminution continued, even accelerated. One time, upon leaving you, when the aides had come to put you to bed, I had forgotten something and had to step back into your room. There, I saw you, in your wheelchair in the middle of the room, with an aide brushing your teeth for you. The look you gave me said, "This is how it is, Daughter, this is how it is." You did not look away but kept looking at me, lovingly, teaching another last lesson. I threw you a kiss, dashed to my car, and broke down sobbing. My once preeminently self-reliant mother could not even brush her own teeth now.

This is how it is, Daughter.

In response to your darkening world, now, side by side with you, I filled the air with words—I became Scheherazade, the mythical storyteller who told stories to keep herself alive, though in our version I was doing so to keep you alive. This is when I adopted the documentary style of storytelling in relating the highlights of your life and our life as a family.

"After the war, when you and Dad settled in Chehalis, you didn't have much money and housing was short, but luckily you found a little house out in the country."

"After your kids left home, you capitalized on all those years you cut our hair—thank you very much again, Mom, for all those great cuts—and you went back to beauty school. After all, with an empty nest, what were you supposed to do? Sit on your duff?"

You nodded. I went on, "Does that sound like you or what?" You smiled, remembering your former feisty self.

With my arm around you, you leaned into me, your head down, tracking my tales, nodding at points meaningful to you, especially the story of you clinging to your father's pants leg when the banker came out to the farm to threaten your dad with foreclosure. "But you survived, Mom," I said, "you survived the Great Depression, didn't you?" You looked up at me and said, "Uh-huh." Then you lowered your head and leaned into me again, listening for more.

Scheherazade kept it up—filling the air with memories and history—in your room, at dinnertime, on our after-dinner "drives" when I wheeled you around the facility for a change of scenery, including a few steps onto the back veranda for a breath of outside air.

On the way home, Scheherazade was quiet—no car radio, no CD. Driving in silence, she thought on her mother's life; she thought on life itself.

To keep you as mobile as possible despite your immobilization, I urged you to wheel yourself around the facility, to give your arms and shoulders some exercise. In ducking that suggestion, you flashed some residual wit.

"I would if I weren't so busy."

I was wheeling you at the time and stopped to laugh quietly into your shoulder. "Mom, who knew you would end up the Queen of Irony?"

"What's that mean?" you asked.

"Irony means saying the opposite of what you really mean."

Your response? "That's lying."

Come to think of it, Mom, perhaps it is. Certainly, we were not in the land of irony now. We were in the Valley of the Shadow of Death, dealing with reality. And it felt good to be with you. Where else would I be?

To keep you as engaged as possible with the world and life, I got us doing jigsaw puzzles in the activities room. You never liked idle hands, and with jigsaw puzzles, our hands were busy, building beautiful pictures. The worried look on your face eased when we were doing our puzzles. I would push a half-dozen pieces of the same color over to you, and you tried to do your part. You were terrible at it, but I told you "Good job" anyway.

In that last year, we did thirteen puzzles, including one of an English country inn and garden, one of an Irish harbor, two of the view from a library looking out, and one of the canals in Venice. You remembered us going to Venice; you remembered me buying a scarf for you from a street vendor. But our favorite puzzles were the three we did of Van Gogh paintings, with our absolute favorite being his "Café Terrace at Night." We kept exclaiming over the light spilling from the café onto the pavement.

Happily, while working the jigsaws, Scheherazade could keep up her storytelling *and* keep one arm around her mother.

The End

See the two women, Mother and Daughter, in the activities room at a table in a corner. At other tables, residents bicker over whose turn it is at cards or proselytize for Jesus, but the two women pay them no attention and quietly work their jigsaw puzzle. Having already worked out the puzzle of their titanic struggle, a jigsaw is just recreation. With one arm around her Mother, the Daughter speaks quietly to her. The Mother leans into her Daughter, listening. They are, these two women, the picture of harmony—the place the Daughter always wanted them to get to. This is the image the Daughter will carry henceforth on her own trek. It is an image, it is a truth, that still amazes her. After much struggle, their earthly bond resolves in such a simple and quiet way.

About four months from the end, as we were working another jigsaw puzzle, when you were dozing more often, I ventured to ask you a big philosophical question. You did not like the big philosophical questions—you preferred ground reality—but I liked them. They get at the deeper truths. As I moved a piece into place—it was another Van Gogh painting, this one of a thatched cottage—I asked: "So, Mom, what do you think of life?"

And you came out of your doze, lifted your head, got very clear, and said: "I think life is wonderful."

Tears sprang to my eyes. "Oh, Momma," I said, "I am *so* glad to hear you say that!"

Mom: I am taking that response—your uncommonly lyrical response—as a *Yes*. . . to life itself and perhaps even to the final trek.

I thank you also for all your expressions of love—"I love you, Sissie"—which I heard constantly toward the end. You said it to me when I arrived for my visit, at dinnertime; you said it when

I wheeled you around the facility; you said it during our jigsaw puzzle time, when you came out of a doze; and of course, you said it when I departed. How wonderful to see you "perk up" at the sight of me when I came into your room or joined you in the dining room. And I was generous with, "I love you, too, Mom."

All this expression of love—I did not tell you this, not even as a joke—I could have used it earlier in my life, during those wilderness years, and no doubt you could have, too. But I was happy, happy, happy to hear it now. I smiled inwardly: Daughter and Mother cashed in their humungous holdings of love at the very end. I think we broke the casino, Mom.

Van Gogh said the artist must have a "warm heart for his fellow man." So must we all.

About this time, four months from the end, I took a break of a few days and joined Larry on the Oregon Coast for a reunion with his siblings. We were at the air and space museum in McMinnville, watching a film about hurricanes on the giant wall-to-wall screen, when—suddenly—I knew in my bones I should *not* be watching a film, I had to leave and get to you, my ailing—my dying—mother. (Talk about metaphor. Hurricanes?) Larry made my excuses to his sibs—"You have to understand about this family"—and explained how Dad, enroute to his dying mother, suddenly knew in his bones that she had just died. Happily, you were still with us, but I felt the spirit and moved.

J.C. had done the same thing a bit earlier, during a vacation with Sue, Miki, and Joe in New Zealand. Suddenly he knew he really-really should *not* be half a world away, larking around, when his mother lay ailing, possibly dying. He begged off from the others and took the long flight home.

The End

On my drive home from Oregon, I called J.C. to share our extrasensory notes. We agreed: There was no question but to act on the feeling. He then spoke of his latest visit with you, Mom, a few days earlier. He said you looked at him for a long time, and tears filled your eyes. "What could *that* mean?"

"Do you want to know what I think, dear brother? With those tears, Mom is saying she is sorry she undervalued you, the joker, all your life—and she is finally acknowledging that it was the troubles between her and Dad that, to save yourself, made you into a joker, a wit. The penny finally dropped; the penny was finally forced to drop. And now that it's too late to make amends, she is saying, 'Sorry.'"

J.C. said that was something to think about. We agreed we had never heard you say sorry; tears at the end would be your way of apology. I repeated what you said about him back in the surgical rehab unit after one of his visits. "That son of mine is quite a guy." He said he regretted there would be no time to follow up on this encouraging note, as I had done.

I said, "Don't lash yourself about what didn't happen, dear brother. Take what did happen—Mom's tears—and be content."

In family, it's all about interpretation, isn't it? I urged my hurting brother to interpret our mother's tears both as regret at not knowing her own son fully and as her late apology. There is so much regret in that, and so much love.

It is comforting to know that, apart from family, you had familiar faces around you your last year. There was Polly from the old neighborhood, whose husband built your house; Polly was in a room around the corner from you. There was Fran, from church, who was directly across the hall. And there was Wilma, mother of J.C.'s childhood friend, Steve. These old friends were your dining partners. Polly, still going strong at 101, after dinner always came around to your wheelchair, placed her hand on your shoulder, leaned close and said, "See you in the mor-ning."

When you died, I went into the dining room to inform them, but Polly could tell what my news was before I announced it. She shook her head and put her hands to her face.

I am glad you had those familiar faces and kind hearts around you at the end. They are all gone now, with Wilma following you by a month, then Polly, then Fran.

About a month from the end, you started to refuse food. As with Dad, you must have known what that meant for the body. Now when I joined you at dinner, where you were quietly carrying out your strike, you nearly always eventually did as I bade: You ate. A little, but at least you ate.

But, of course, I could not deny the significance of your strike.

Later one evening during this period, when I was at the gym speed-walking, trying to de-stress, an ancient memory came back to me, not my memory but the one you enjoyed relating to me throughout my life . . . you, as a young mother, protecting me, your infant daughter, from a tornado, by lying on top of me in a ditch at the edge of a field in Texas. *How*, I prayed, *how can I protect my mother from the tornado coming at her?*

Then, it hit me, and I stopped stock still on the track. *Mom is ready for the tornado.*

As I said in my eulogy, about protecting you from the final tornado, "Of course, staying real, as Mom always did . . . It cannot happen; death must come."

About two weeks from the end, your calcium count spiked, and Ted urged the facility to send you to the hospital. You were there almost a week, visibly failing. When you were moved back to the facility, you were on an oxygen machine. You slept all your last week. Aides needed to turn you every hour or so to avoid bedsores. There was no more talking. The last time I heard your voice was in the hospital.

Your family was with you constantly. I came down every day of your last two weeks. Larry drove down almost as often.

That last week, in the quiet of your room, the oxygen machine pumping, your life ebbing away, it sounds strange to say, but I loved being in that room with you. I moved back and forth between the table where I worked a last jigsaw puzzle in your honor—of a farm scene, the setting of your childhood—and your bed, where another kind of puzzle was working out, where I held your hand, smoothed your cheek, repeated in your ear, "I love you" and "I'm so proud of us, Mom." It all felt . . . sacred.

On the night before you died, Sunday night, after staying longer than usual, I gathered my things to go, but something told me to stay even longer. I set my things down, went over to the forest of family photos on your dresser, and picked up the framed photos of Dad and your parents. I took them to your bedside and sat down.

The hospice nurse had said that, though you were comatose, you could still hear. I don't know if you heard me, but, alone with you, I bade my Farewell. It was like one of our ultraviolet moments, Mom, where everything coming out of our mouths was true and loaded with maximum meaning, only this time it was one-way.

"Momma," I said. "Something is telling me this is probably goodbye; something is telling me this is the last time I will talk to you. In my hands I am holding a photo of Dad, the one I took back in college that you always liked so much because it showed up his blue eyes. You'll soon be seeing Dad again. He will be so happy to see you, Mom. He loved you so, so much. There was never anyone else for him but you. And I have a photo of your beloved parents. They will be so glad to greet their daughter again. And don't you worry about your daughter, Mom. I will carry on *because* I am your daughter. I am strong and proud and resilient and stubborn, like you. I have at my side the best possible husband and partner, Larry. And don't worry about my cancer, I have modern medicine on my side, too. I will be okay . . .

"And about the miracle you and I pulled off. We were lost to each other for so long, Momma, but, thank God, we found each other again. We worked out the problems between us and, guess what? We found out we were both right. We both had good reasons for thinking what we thought, doing what we did. I led the way back, but you stuck with me throughout our journey. I got my mother's trust back. And you got your daughter's love back.

"Mom, I cannot tell you how proud I am of us. *This* is how I will carry on: knowing we, you and I, worked a miracle. Bless you, Mom. Thank you for giving me life. Thank you for our renewed bond. I will see you again someday. Not soon, I hope, because I have so much work to do yet. But when it comes my time, I will embrace you in joy. I love you with all my heart, Mom. God bless you."

I kissed you on the forehead and drove home in silence. I knew.

The next day, Larry was in the room with you, along with Ted and Jan, when Jan noticed, from the oxygen machine, you were no longer breathing. Earlier Larry had called to pass on what the hospice nurse had said, that you were actively dying and death would come anytime in the next few days. I grabbed at that promise of extra time. But you departed earlier. I was on the Narrows Bridge when Larry called.

"Dear, your mother has just died."

"Oh," I said, "the hour is come." I looked south from atop the bridge, down the passage where the early explorers sailed through centuries ago, and I envisioned your spirit passing over. "Bless your soul, Mom." When I got to you, my first words were not about lamenting not getting to you in time, but relief. "I am so, so glad we moved back out here seventeen years ago."

The first days after you left this world, Mom, I was constantly in tears, haunted, overcome by the look of fear on your face in your last year, you who were fearless in life. How awful, how frightening was your passage?

The condolence notes streamed in. One, from Larry's former seatmate in the legislature, Patricia, contained a poem by Emily Dickinson which I had not known but spoke to the leaden moment. "The Bustle in a House / The Morning after Death / Is solemnest of industries / Enacted upon Earth." And this line of Emily's, from my favorite poem of hers, came to me repeatedly. "This World is not Conclusion . . ."

Viewing your body at the funeral home brought more tears. A strand of your hair had come loose from your bun and lay—out of its proper place!—on the pillow, a sight that broke my heart again. I sobbed as I tucked the strand back in, to restore you to your normal well-groomed state. With that gesture, I became aware I was the only one crying; your sons and our excellent spouses were managing their feelings. But why manage heartbreak? Later I said, attempting some lightness, "You know, you guys might try crying. It's good to express your feelings."

But of course, as Millie's daughter, I needed to manage. Also, I had to get organized, because I was designated organizer of your memorial service. Which you, ever organized, made easy. We found the folder marked "Funeral Arrangements" exactly where you told us. In it, translating your left-hand slant, I discovered your obituary, which you had helpfully written, leaving the death date blank. I came across slips of paper with your favorite hymns, your favorite passages of scripture, even a poem, all of which made it into your service. Several times in your notes you reminded us—clearly a nagging concern for you—"Don't forget to pay the organist!"

Getting organized, that first weekend I sat down to take notes for my eulogy to you and, no surprise, I got carried along and wrote the whole thing in one ever-unfurling wave. Not to worry, I adhered by your guidance to your eulogists, which you stated repeatedly in your notes. "No mush."

But again, Mom, there is such a thing as honest feeling. Perhaps its expression is my contribution to the family?

Your service went well. The church was packed with the familiar faces who remain; their children, now adults, also came, sometimes as envoys for their dearly departed parents. My childhood friends Claire and Annie came; Brian and John called; Jack, Karen, Dorothy emailed. J.C.'s childhood friend Bob made your famous Finnish coffee cake for the reception. Your dictum of "No mush" notwithstanding, there were tears for you. Mostly, though, there was a great swell of love for Millie.

Importantly, crucially, the feeling I soon got, and suffuses me still, is this: Oceanic love for you, Mom. That is the word I used with Larry days after your death. "My love for Mom is—what is a big enough word?—oceanic. I have never felt this way about my mother before. I feel so blessed."

Conversely—I know I should keep counting my blessings and not "go there"—I can't help occasionally going back to our early years to that suffering child, so unhappy and frightened. How she could have used even a drop of this oceanic love now swirling in her. The contrast between then and now is so great that, once in a while, the mind just has to exclaim. I tell the suffering child I once was, "It got better, it really did. Categorically better."

Much as I luxuriate now in this oceanic love for you, I did have one dark night of the soul after your death and, yes, it related to that suffering child I once was. It occurred three months after you died. I was watching the English film, *The Go-Between*. I had avoided the film when it first came out, in 1971, and, though I had bought the novel by L.P. Hartley, I never read it. From the title, this former go-between could tell what the story was about. Now, all these years later, and with our miraculous reunion now achieved, I surely was fortified to examine, with new objectivity, the circumstances of my childhood, wasn't I? Not so; not so at all.

The film is about a boy, twelve years old, who comes for a stay with the wealthy family of a school chum. He becomes infatuated with the friend's beautiful older sister and seeks to ingratiate himself with her. She, though engaged to the son of another wealthy family, has conceived a passion for a rugged local farmer. To conduct this illicit affair, she needs a go-between to carry messages, and finds an eager volunteer in the boy. But the heat of the proceedings is far beyond what the boy can handle, and his agonized face in extended close-ups spun me back to my childhood. That boy was me, of course. The film ends with the boy, now middle-aged and a scarred shell of a man, obliging once again the woman who, oblivious to any injury she inflicted on him years before, asks him once again to act as go-between, this time taking a message to the estranged grandson of the son she had by the farmer.

I did not sleep that night. I sat up, flashing on the boy's agonized face, the cruelty of the clueless "adults" who used him as a sacrificial lamb. Next day I could not write; my heart pounded so hard, I headed to the gym to walk off the wild churning. As I walked toward the gym, I experienced a crescendo of anger at my own users—my parents, who after all were medical people. *Did they not see the injury they were inflicting on me?* I was sweating torrents, my heart was thundering in my ears. Was I going into shock, having a stroke?

To rescue myself, I did what I have done before to save my life. I visualized throwing another grenade at my feet—this time to stop the flow of fury at my parents. *Stop it, stop it, stop it!* I shouted to myself. (I may have shouted this out loud.) *No more suffering! No more suffering for this family! You are done, done, done with suffering for this family—do you hear? Yes, your parents should have stopped the suffering, but they didn't. But you will—now!*

It worked! I got calm; my breathing became regular. As I resumed walking, I understood.

My forgiveness of you had been articulated, but not yet felt. But now it was felt, it was hammered into my heart. I also understood I had to forgive Dad, too. Just as, I reminded myself, you two had forgiven me.

Since that near-breakdown in the gym parking lot, there have been no more. Should there be, I will tell myself, *I have more grenades in my arsenal.* And I will instruct myself, *No more suffering. You are done, done, done with suffering for this family, do you hear?*

Soon after that, I was driving home at dusk, east to west. As I headed down the long slope approaching the Narrows Bridge, the beautiful vista ahead—of our tree-filled peninsula, the Olympic Mountains in the distance, the vista that drew Larry and me to put down stakes—was lit up by a spectacular sunset: pink, orange, red.

"Oh, Mom," I said, out loud, "you would *love* this sunset."

Envisioning you in the passenger seat and moving to take your hand as I often did when we went out for a drive, I now put my hand down on your seat—*and the seat was warm!*

"Mom?" I said.

It took me a second to figure it out. The seat warmer had been left on. I laughed. I laughed again when I remembered that evening was our favorite time of day, yours and mine.

"You really pick your metaphors, Mom," I said.

When I got home, I told Larry about the Miracle of the Seat Warmer. I also said, "I really need to stop this talking out loud to Mom. People will wonder . . ."

Part Five

The
Beginning

I can hear you saying now, "Time to wrap this up." I agree. Time to wrap up our story, time to wrap up the grieving, time to fix on the world again.

How wonderful that, going forward—the direction Americans always want to go—you go with me, because I *can* hear you now.

Our story has taken me five months to write, from mid-fall to early spring. Just last weekend we switched our clocks ahead an hour. Chiming the time in our house now is the grandfather clock Dad assembled, such a lovely deep tone. The grieving has given way to warm thoughts, warm memories. The large framed photo of you that we placed on the church altar for your memorial service looks down on me as I write; it has presided over the telling of our story; I smile at you, on us.

On the first anniversary of your death, J.C. called. The son who had held in so much about you talked away for an hour and a half. Ted, your designated executor, executed well. We had teased him that Mr. Casual came to our estate-settlement meetings with a big binder of documents, complete with color tabs.

Larry says he still gets it in mind to "go see Mom," then realizes, *Hmmm*, he can't.

Meanwhile, the world has taken startling dark turns, accelerating an ominous trend toward autocracy and strongman rule, away from democracy. The proto-autocratic Mr. Trump is not the only problem; autocrats the world over have adapted the tools of liberal democracy and turned them to their own illiberal ends—rigging elections, "reforming" judiciaries, jailing journalists and opponents—all in pursuit of the eternal Holy Grail: power. For a commentator, there is no end of material. For small-d democrats, there is no end to urgency. It's all-hands-on-deck time. Larry and I do not plan to retire; we can't.

In commentary, I have been making the case that America is in a grand reckoning, not a breakdown. Counterforces to breakdown manifest all over; John Q. Public has gotten off his sofa. It broke your heart, you said, to see America "sliding down" these last decades. The only counter to slide is to reckon and to rebuild. I believe this, not only because of the life credo I subscribed to long ago from the Roman poet Virgil: "Easy is the descent to the lower depths; but to retrace your steps and to escape to the upper air—this is the task, this is the toil." But I also believe it because *we* were in breakdown, Mom, you and I, but we reckoned and we rebuilt, and we got to a New Day. One brings to the table, to the battle, one's lived experience—in our case, experience hard-earned—and one deals from there.

Because we got to a New Day, you and I, you got to a new place of contentment. I am thinking now of the time, shortly after we got past the major negotiations of "the main event" fifteen years ago, when I was talking to a friend who knew of our past troubles. In an ultraviolet moment of truth telling, I surprised myself by saying to him, "I don't think my mother ever thought she could be so happy." You always bore hardship well, but your soul was unquiet. Now, because of our miracle, you got to enjoy a lightness of being. To the end, I may have mystified you, but we fascinated each other, a mix that—I can hear you saying this!—"kept it interesting."

The Beginning

For myself, because we got to a New Day, I get to bask in oceanic love for you. Gone is the sorrowful heart whenever I thought of my mother. I now get to embrace her in all her being (except for her political views). Too, I get to claim the traits that made you distinctly you—your pragmatism, directness, no-airs realness. I used to resist acknowledging it, but we are so alike: tenacious, looking for room to maneuver, and, most importantly, sturdy morally—we *both* win! And because of the miracle we worked, I get to believe that tragedy can be averted, used as grist for transformation, I get to believe in Renaissance. In Italian, "renaissance" (*rinascimento*) means rebirth. That states it perfectly—about you and me, about America.

And the miracle that will fuel me the rest of my earthly trek: I get to keep talking to you. Where once the line between us was jammed, now it is open and the signal is clear. This is not goodbye, Mom. This is hello. Indeed, this World is *not* Conclusion.

Two women—Mother and Daughter—get into a car, the Mother taking the wheel. The Mother appears as the Daughter remembers her from their early years—beautiful, vivacious, healthy. The Daughter appears as she is now.

DAUGHTER
You look quite chic [pronounced "chick"].

MOTHER
Thank you. I feel good. They're still not doing your hair right. I cut it better.

DAUGHTER
That is true, that is true.

Across the Kitchen Table

MOTHER
Now then: Where to, Daughter?

The Daughter pauses, looks out at the darkening world. Then back to her Mother.

DAUGHTER
Anywhere, Mom. Anywhere.

Acknowledgments

With a memoir, which is drawn from life, the author could acknowledge any number of members of the human parade encountered on the Road of Life. But that listing, while rich, would be endless. To focus solely on the writing of this memoir, the citations are fewer and more select.

First, of course, I acknowledge my late mother, Mildred Gwen Morgan Lofberg. In a way, from beyond the grave, Mom has been my co-author, as the recipient of this letter-as-memoir. Not only was Mom the author of my being, but she was my early moral arbiter. As such, in her struggle with my father, whose defense I took up, our struggle—the one between Mom and me—became a moral one. In that No Man's Land between my parents, I see, in a way I never saw before writing this memoir, that I forged my moral character there. It is my life's greatest feat to have broken the impasse existing so many decades between Mom and me and to have rebuilt—together—our primal bond.

Then there is my dear husband, Larry, who throughout my writing career has served as First Reader and who read this memoir as it poured out of me, part by part. Importantly, Second Reader is our best friend Dr. Joseph G. Bell. Joe knew and loved Mom and pronounced this rendering of our story a "valentine."

And there are my two brothers, J.C. ("J") and Ted, who read with keen interest what I had shielded them from in our early family life and who were magnanimous and thoughtful in their response.

Also key are the early readers of a manuscript. I thank my writer friends Linda Barrett Osborne and Elizabeth Murray for their warm writerly response, as well as my regular nonwriter friends who read it: Eileen Pestorius, Dr. Lisa Plymate, and Barbara Squires.

I thank my former literary agent, Anne Dubuisson, of the former Ellen Levine agency in New York City. Anne pointed me to She Writes Press, feeling we would be "a good fit."

Finally, I must again acknowledge my mother. After decades of near-zero trust between us, Mom placed her full trust in me to lead us to harmony; she came to believe in my determination we would not end in tragedy. If that meant we had to unpack this and traverse that from our contentious past, she never "bucked," she stayed with me all the way. What greater gift could I have—my mother's love *and* trust, my best benediction—as I continue down the Road of Life? In my kit-bag with me is my most precious provision—*our* story.

About the Author

Carla Seaquist (1944-2024) was an author and playwright who focused her commentary after the 9/11 attacks on politics, culture, and ethical-moral issues. Venues for her commentary have been (in order) *The Christian Science Monitor, HuffPost*, and *Medium*. Two volumes of her collected commentary—*Can America Save Itself from Decline?*—have been published, with Volume III due out Spring 2025. Her first book is titled, *Manufacturing Hope: Post-9/11 Notes on Politics, Culture, Torture, and the American Character.* Renowned investigative reporter Seymour Hersh calls Seaquist "an essayist in the great American tradition."

Her play *Who Cares?: The Washington-Sarajevo Talks*, based on her calls with a man under siege in Sarajevo, received its premiere at Chicago's Victory Gardens Theater, with subsequent productions at Washington's Studio Theatre and the Festival of Emerging American Theater. This play, along with *Kate and Kafka*, was published as *Two Plays of Life and Death.*

Seaquist's early career was in civil rights. She organized the women's caucus at the Brookings Institution, Washington, DC, and served as Equal Opportunity Officer for the City of San Diego, for which she received NOW's Susan B. Anthony award. She served on the California Governor's Task Force on Civil Rights and the board of Humanities Washington. Majoring in international relations, Seaquist earned a BA, *cum laude*, from American University's School of International Service and pursued an MA at Johns Hopkins School of Advanced International Studies, with one year in Bologna, Italy. She was married to Larry Seaquist, a retired US Navy captain and former Washington state legislator, now an educator and writer. After long-time residence in Washington, DC, she and Larry returned to live and work in Gig Harbor in "the other Washington."

Her work is archived on her website,
www.carlaseaquist.com.

Looking for your next great read?

We can help!

Visit www.shewritespress.com/next-read
or scan the QR code below for a list
of our recommended titles.

She Writes Press is an award-winning
independent publishing company founded to
serve women writers everywhere.